The Human Geography of
Contemporary Britain

The Human Geography of Contemporary Britain

Edited by

John R. Short
University of Reading

and

Andrew Kirby
University of Colorado at Boulder

MACMILLAN

First published in this format 1984 by
Higher and Further Education Division
MACMILLAN PUBLISHERS LTD
Houndsmills, Basingstoke,
Hampshire, RG21 2XS,
and London
Companies and representatives
throughout the world

ISBN 0 333 37315 4 (hard cover)
ISBN 0 333 37316 2 (paperback)

Typeset by
Wessex Typesetters Ltd
Frome, Somerset

Printed in Hong Kong

British Library Cataloguing in Publication Data
The human geography of contemporary Britain.
1. Anthropo-geography—Great Britain
I. Short, John R.   II. Kirby, Andrew
304.2′0941   GF551
ISBN 0–333–37315–4
ISBN 0–333–37316–2 Pbk

Contents

6 Contents

List of Figures

List of Tables

9

10 *List of Tables*

1
Britain in Transition

John R. Short and Andrew Kirby

In 1969 *The Geographical Magazine* published a series of articles under the broad title of 'Resources for Britain's Future', which subsequently appeared in book form (Chisholm, 1972). The tone of the articles reflected the tenor of the times: they were imbued with an optimism in continued economic growth tempered by a concern with the proper use of resources. The dominant themes were the problems of guiding and controlling economc growth in a small densely populated country with finite resources. Times have changed. We have witnessed the end of the post-war boom, reductions in government welfare expenditure and the emergence of private affluence with the threat of public squalor. Economic growth is no longer assured and this realisation has caused the reassessment of many accepted views and beliefs. Full employment has been difficult to obtain and has been all but jettisoned as a government aim; regional policy has been cruelly undermined by economic trends and in the inner areas of our major cities the problems of multiple deprivation continue to persist. The picture is, however, not entirely one of unrelieved gloom. Since the 1970s there have been rising standards of living and, on the whole, people in Britain are now better off than they have been in the past. However, in the context of rising expectations this general affluence has tended to highlight the disparities in our society: between regions, between races, between urban and rural dwellers, and between home-owners and tenants. These divisions overlie and sometimes exacerbate the traditional disparities between different socio-economic groups.

These problems are now being studied by human geographers. The most valuable research in British human geography is concerned with three main themes. First, there is the exploration of issues which illuminate the conflicts in society. These exist in many contexts – housing, transportation, recreation and land-use in general. Second, there has been an associated theme of assessing the redistributional consequences of public policies, social processes and spatial structures. The questions of 'who gets what, where and why' and 'who gains and who loses' are becoming pivotal points in contemporary human geography. Third, there have been various attempts to understand the processes which generate, maintain and change patterns of conflict and inequality. An important strand here has been the explicit analysis of the state and an evaluation of the impact of public policy. This research has involved a concern for processes as well as pattern, qualitative and quantitative approaches, inter-disciplinary awareness and an increasing maturity towards the examination of social issues.

It was against this intellectual and social background that we asked certain active scholars to write articles for a series in *The Geographical Magazine* entitled 'The Human Geography of Contemporary Britain'. The series was published in 1981–2. These articles have been revised and updated for this present volume. Taken as a whole they provide a coherent survey of the main elements of the human geography of Britain. Underlying the chapters are three themes:

1. The slowing down of economic growth and associated spatial outcomes
2. The changing role and diverse functions of the state
3. The nature of new conflicts and emerging social tensions

which we will now discuss.

Industrial Change and Spatial Outcomes

Major changes have occurred in the main employment sectors of manufacturing and services in recent years. The former has declined from 37 to 50 per cent of total employment while the latter has grown from 48 to 59 per cent between 1955 and 1980. As David Keeble argues, these shifts have not happened at the same speed and in the same way in all locations. Terms like 'core' and 'periphery' have often been employed in an attempt to identify the forces that dictate spatial patterns of growth, decline and change.

As Keeble shows, however, even these spatial reference points shift and alter. In the early 1970s, a general convergence appeared to be taking place within the British economy, with unemployment in 'the regions' falling, and other indicators – such as female participation – moving towards the national mean.

This is initially surprising, as it was in areas like the North East, the North West, Central Scotland and Wales that major manufacturing losses were greatest. The major interventions of the state were of course crucial in offsetting this decline, with all the threats that it would pose to the operation of local economies and indeed the legitimacy of the state itself, a point developed at length by Peter Taylor and Ron Johnston. Thus although a large proportion of 1.7 million jobs lost between 1955 and 1980 were in the periphery, the best estimates are that some 400,000 jobs were in turn created by various state subsidies. These were principally dispensed via regional policy, although job creation slowed as economic and fiscal crises began to emerge in 1976, and faltered as regional aid was badly cut after 1979.

This is not to suggest that traditional disparities between the core and the financially assisted regions were disappearing. Many of the jobs created in the 1960s and 1970s were poorly paid and demanded low skills. Female labour was attracted into branch plants offering part-time jobs in routine tasks, while in areas like the South East and East Anglia firms consolidated their office functions, advertising accounts and research and development units, all offering more satisfying skilled employment with commensurately higher pay.

More important, the different regions proved after 1977 to have very different job stability. Unemployment rates at the regional scale, which had been converging, began quite quickly to diverge again as the lowly branch plants were closed down and more traditional industries continued to close shipyards, steel plants or assembly shops. Various factors were responsible. Unplanned rises in energy costs were a constant factor throughout advanced economies in the 1970s, but as Peter Odell shows, Britain had a particularly confused energy policy and was unprepared for such shocks. In addition, there were more specific changes in the traditional patterns of operation of the economy. Longstanding links with Commonwealth countries were eroded by their increase of indigenous production. Other new industrial producers – notably

Japan – lengthened their stride and began to dominate the market in highly profitable sectors like automobiles and technological hardware throughout the EEC. Within Britain itself, contractions within the nationalised industries (many of which are large employers and consumers of others' products) also served to fuel the downward demand spiral.

As Massey and Meegan (1982) have shown in detail, British industrial capital has responded – albeit belatedly – to this crisis of profitability by attempting to rationalise production. This has taken three forms, notably employment contraction/intensification; mergers and rationalisation; and technical change. All three have taken place in the past, although low-level changes such as the speeding-up of production lines have been more usual. More drastic changes are now more common. Industrial structures are being rationalised, which usually means that marginal plants are closed down. Similarly, technical change is likely to be concentrated in the key plants, particularly where employment structures are receptive to such deskilling. The 'modern firm' has two very different needs *vis-à-vis* its labour. Headquarters and R & D functions require an internalised labour force which can be trained and groomed as required. The productive capacity, however, only requires the basic assembly skills, even when advanced equipment is being produced. Consequently local economies with pools of (part-time) labour and weakly developed employment practices are most desirable: there may even be advantages in keeping the two parts of the company apart, as this will further inhibit unionisation.

The net result of these structural changes is a spatial economy which has been characterised as 'New Britain' and 'Traditional Britain' (Donnison and Soto, 1980). Away from the core (which is, crudely, the Norwich–Bristol axis), we find local economies characterised by very high levels of external control (i.e. from outside the region or even outside the UK); declining male and increasing female employment profiles; and very low levels of research and development. In the North West, for example, the nine largest firms in the region all have their headquarters outside the area, and as elsewhere, major rationalisations, mergers and contractions have taken place, with GEC and British Leyland, for example, closing down major plants in Trafford Park (Manchester) and Speke (Liverpool). However, even indigenous firms can afford no loyalty to their locality: Tootal (textiles), for instance, have shed over 7,000 jobs in the North West, but created over 14,000 elsewhere in the world. The net result of 'rationalisation' is of course three million cases of registered unemployment in 1983.

One of the reasons why unemployment has risen so rapidly in places like the West Midlands and the North West is that the industrial structure seems incapable of rapidly generating new jobs. External control, as we have noted, means few centres of innovation. However, even indigenous firms seem to be characterised by low levels of innovation and product growth: in the North East, even among independent companies, more than half had not developed a new product in over five years. The importance of technology in both regional and urban change is more fully explored by John Goddard in Chapter 4.

The state's response to these changes within the economy has been characterised by contradictions. As we have noted, contractions within the nationalised industries have undermined the attempts to build up local economies within the Assisted Areas. The state is, however, constrained to pursue its regional policies, in order to maintain its legitimacy. Similarly, attempts have been made to stimulate local economies where the high costs of labour reproduction and falling consumption are seen to be unacceptable: as Bob Bennett demonstrates, high unemployment, the need for social services and a declining tax base can produce serious local political problems. In the past, we have witnessed the construction of explicit growth poles (such as Washington New Town), although it can be argued that this in turn contradicts other arms of state activity, such as policy directed towards neighbouring inner cities.

The rationalisation of industrial capital has, because of its speed, produced an unacceptably high level of human wastage. It is also clear that the state has contributed to this process, with the channelling of funds into 'efficient' and 'effective' firms (50 per cent of all regional aid in 1975 went into the construction of four oil terminals in Scotland). It has also encouraged rationalisation in its own sectors, such as British Leyland, British Aerospace and British Airways. At present, the surplus generated by oil revenues has permitted the state to maintain its legitimacy; but how long this can continue is a moot point. Recent events have created a geographical pattern of advantage and disadvantage that will become frozen and entrenched for a generation to come.

The Political Scene

The political scene in mainland Britain has been dominated by the experience of economic decline. This slowing-down of growth and the increasing of unemployment have been the pivotal point for political discourse. We can identify three major responses.

Political parties

First, there has been the response of the political parties. Since the mid-1960s the Conservative party has responded to the decline by questioning the post-war consensus, the corporate compromise between government, big capital and organised labour involving Keynesian demand management and relatively high levels of welfare expenditure. In both 1970 and 1979 Conservative governments came to power on slogans of returning to market forces. The Heath government was stopped by the power of organised labour and there was a mid-term U-turn. However, the drift to the right in Conservative thinking continued during their years of opposition, and Thatcherism emerged in the 1970s as a mixture of a belief in a strong state with emphasis on law and order and defence, and an economic doctrine which saw the public sector as a burden on the real economy. The government's aims were to reduce inflation and to ensure the return of market forces to a dominant position in the economy. These were to be combined with a strong anti-union rhetoric and a desire to freeze organised labour out of the corporate triangle. The economic underpinning of Thatcherism was an attempt to improve the position of capital *vis-à-vis* labour in the belief that this would regenerate the British economy.

The Labour party when in government between 1974 and 1979 responded to the economic crisis with policies pursuing public expenditure reductions (in retrospect this can be seen as a mild preface to Thatcherism), and an incomes policy. The revolt of rank and file union members against what they saw as too restrictive a pay policy led, in the 'winter of discontent' of 1978–9, to the fall of the Labour party. Thereafter, the experience of the first Thatcher government led to a re-evaluation of Labourism; what emerged from the crucible of debate was a reiteration of the beneficial effects of government spending in a recession and a further commitment to democratisation in the community and workplace. There was also a further radicalisation of the grass roots as party workers sought to control the parliamentary representatives. The underlying belief was that the Labour party in office had been more corporatist than socialist.

For many, these trends in the major parties were seen as increased polarisation. Many of those on the right of the Labour party and the left of the Conservative party saw themselves as being the only ones in the traditional centre ground of British politics. It was from this general perspective that the SDP party was founded and the alliance with the Liberal party was formed. With over 20 per cent of the votes cast in the 1983 election the alliance constitutes an important political force, but one whose power is blunted by the facts of electoral representation. The alliance support is wide but, given the British first-past-the-post system, not deep enough to turn votes into seats. They have no spatial equivalent to the Tory shire counties or Labour urban strongholds.

Politics and civil society

There has also been the response of the populace to formal politics. In terms of voting behaviour we can notice a general decline in votes cast for the major political parties. No government since the mid-1960s has been returned with a majority of votes cast. The main reason for this decline in instrumental voting has been the perceived inability of the major political parties to deal with the economic crisis. Here we have an interesting ambivalence. While many people have enjoyed an increase in their standards of living, this is seen as a result of individual effort and endeavour, but the slowing-down of the economy (as shown in macro-economic indicators) has been seen as indicating the failure of government. There has not been a crisis of legitimation: rather a steady decline in the belief that politicians can solve Britain's economic ills.

Voting patterns have not been uniform throughout the country. As Taylor and Johnston show, the swing to the Conservatives since the mid-1960s has a definite spatial bias, with the greatest swings being recorded in suburban and shire counties. The swing has been much smaller in urban and industrial areas. Here the appeal to social market forces has far less purchase. This political geography in turn helps to shape government's economic strategy. Not being reliant on the urban-industrial vote and with few political representatives in traditional Britain, the Conservative government can pursue social market strategies which may lead to increased unemployment in the traditional Labour voting areas.

One of the most notable expressions of public opinion was when young people in certain inner-city areas rioted in 1980 and 1981. This was not in itself a reasoned political statement, but in the words of the Scarman report it was the voice of protest whose roots lay in youth unemployment, restricted opportunities and appalling young-black/police relations. The riots were an indication of some of the social costs of Thatcherism.

Public policies in an era of retrenchment

Public policies are being devised and to some extent implemented in a climate of opinion dominated by two trends. First there has been an attempt to control public expenditure. This has been a major theme since the mid-1970s. The attempt to cap spending pro- grammes has not been an easy one. Departmental inertia, existing commitments and the strength of various lobbies all tend to work against the easy implementation of government cutbacks. It has not been a blanket attempt to reduce but rather to redirect expenditure. Under the previous Labour government (and increasingly under the Conservatives) attempts have been made to reduce welfare expenditure but to maintain and increase spending on law and order and defence. Second, there has been an attempt to restructure social policy since 1979 in order to 'reassert individualism, self-reliance and family responsibility, and to reverse the collective social provision of the post-war era' (Gough, 1983, p. 155).

The exact implementation of these general aims into specific policy areas has differed. Although different policy areas share a common context, the varying interests and articulation of general tendencies produce a varied pattern, with restructuring being more successful in some sectors than others, and expenditure reductions being more vigorously pursued in some but not all. It is not a case that all policy sectors exhibit the same degree of expenditure reduction and policy redirection. The variety of public policy responses is highlighted in most of the chapters. Bob Bennett's chapter, for example, shows how party politics plays a major role in policy implementation. The Rate Support Grant was used by the previous Labour government to aid urban areas, while the Conservative government of 1979 shifted the distribution to favour their shire county heartland.

The precise form of the more recent redirection of social policies can be seen in respect to transport and housing. David Banister shows how there has been a sharp reappraisal of public transport with a growing emphasis on reducing subsidy and encouraging market forces. The effects, as he suggests, will in all likelihood be socially regressive. It is not, however, a blanket attack on subsidies. As John R. Short shows, the encouragement of owner-occupation, the one constant of British housing policy of the past twenty years, implies continued exchequer support. Tax relief on mortgage interest and capital gains tax exemption afforded to owner-occupiers amounted to just over £5,000m in 1981–2. It thus appears that subsidies are handouts when given to the poor or in public programmes without government favour. When given to middle income groups to pursue consumption patterns in line with government thinking, they are encouragements to 'self-reliance and family responsibility'.

Public policies and policy implementation are as riven with tension as the underlying ideology is marked by inconsistencies. There is, as Bennett's chapter indicates, an emerging conflict between central and local government, as the former seeks to restrict the expenditure of the latter. The conflict is not simply between central and local, but essentially between the goals of capital accumulation and legitimation split between the two levels of government. The tension cuts across party lines. Not only is the Labour-dominated Association of Metropolitan Authorities against centralised control but so is the Conservative-controlled Association of District Councils. At the district council's annual conference in June 1983 the chairman called on Conservatives to lobby MPs against government plans to impose controls on rate levies. It was a fight, he noted, against the undermining of the autonomy and accountability of local authorities. As the calls for social expenditure reductions increase so will the rift between central and local government.

Since the state is involved in so many facets and has many, often contradictory, goals, implementation of one policy may work against the desired aims of other policies. Encouraging owner-occupation, for example, is likely to produce an increasing number of people with both emotional and material interests in their local area. Labour mobility may be reduced and the emergence of local pressure groups is likely, all fighting against the government encouragement of growth in all its forms. Government policies do not form a coherent programme. As a whole they reflect the often contradictory roles and functions of government. Moreover, the state can and does get it wrong. Peter Odell, for example, argues that the government's energy policies are inappropriate and damaging to the economy. The state is as prone to error as any other major organisation. The state is as riven with tension as the society in which it functions. The state is an arena for disputes, not a solution for them.

New Conflicts

From our preceding remarks, it can be seen that successive governments have interpreted the role of the state to be to maintain the preconditions for capital accumulation, and to oversee social reproduction. Since 1976, little has been done to create employment; instead a succession of strategies has been directed to the amelioration of the resultant poverty and hardship.

Those living in regions such as the North East or North West, Central Scotland and Wales, those with limited job skills, many elderly people and those who in general are economically weak, are facing bleak prospects. None the less, there is little evidence that these groups are explicitly reacting politically to the fact that some regions' residents and the highly skilled in general are maintaining an improvement in their real incomes, albeit a slow one.

The reasons for this are complex. A major reason is that welfare provision maintains standards of life above a base level. In addition, widespread crises of legitimation within the periphery have been avoided by the targeting of financial assistance to specific locations: originally growth poles like New Towns, and latterly to inner areas, where funding has been directed to social services, recreational and housing provision. Whether this expenditure has managed to cosmeticise the rapidly widening gaps between New and Traditional Britain – between those in the inner cities and those in the suburbs, between black and white – remains to be seen. What is clear is that more traditional political responses are shifting.

In the first instance, the locus of the workplace is no longer an automatic determinant of political attitudes. Much employment is now in activities without a union history; more women are employed, who have also been historically excluded from such struggles. Important too is the fact that trades unions are taking wide political issues on board: nuclear disarmament is one example.

Second, the political parties, which have served to reflect petrified class stances over recent decades, have also changed. The Centre-Left has split and is reforming itself into three parties – Liberal, SDP and Labour – which will ultimately cover a wide political spectrum, perhaps of the sort found in countries like Italy or France. The Right is much more narrowly defined, and is represented by a Conservative party which has very rapidly recast itself as a force for limited social expenditure, home-ownership and business values.

Third, and perhaps most significant, there is some evidence that political energies are being redirected into new channels. As Knox and Kirby observe, local political struggles over issues like education are more frequent and are treated as 'real politics'. Often, these struggles are directed towards consumption issues – social services, planning decisions, expenditure cuts. Often, too, they become reified as locational conflicts, with rural areas fighting off the externalities sent their way by the metropolitan areas, as Malcolm Moseley indicates. At other times, neighbouring communities can find themselves in conflict, perhaps over road routes, while in celebrated cases, whole counties may activate themselves against some proposal such as an airport development.

It is always difficult to estimate what these episodic outbursts mean for an understanding of British politics. On the one hand, it is clear that 'the politics of rejection', as practised by many residents' groups, are often less to do with conservation and aesthetics than house prices and neighbourhood reputations. On the other hand, the politicisation of issues broadly based around environmental concerns is proceeding rapidly, as Tim O'Riordan demonstrates. Quite why ecology has entered the popular consciousness is difficult to determine. It may represent a whimsical wish to return to the bucolic fantasy of the advertiser's dream, in which brown bread and real ale are consumed in a virgin setting. Conversely, the fact that a majority in Britain was in 1983 opposed to the introduction of

Cruise missiles indicates that broad issues – nuclear weapons/nuclear power/environmental safety – could be developing as coherent concerns.

These changes will not necessarily add up to a total redrawing of the electoral map, a shift away from national politics and a growing concern with issues of conscience and morality. There is, however, a recognition perhaps that the individual can exert little power against the ideological machinery of the state or the corporate power of multinational capital. For this reason, local issues and environmental questions can increasingly appear as arenas within which voices can be heard and decisions changed.

The Future

The future, as someone noted, is important because we are going to spend the rest of our lives there. While all the chapters consider the present and look to the future, Peter Hall considers in his analysis of the geography of intervention the possible future human geography of Britain. His chapter provides a direct contrast in the treatment of the state and the basis of state action to the chapter by Taylor and Johnston. The difference encapsulates the gulf between liberal and marxist/neo-marxist views of the state.

Hall's vision of a neotechnic Britain is a contentious one. But the future is not predetermined. If we don't like the vision we can in our different ways try to change its realisation.

2
The Geography of the British State

P. J. Taylor and R. J. Johnston

The modern world-economy is divided politically into more than 150 separate sovereign states. Each of these claims sole sovereignty over a particular territorial area, plus, where relevant, adjacent marine and air space. Recognition of a state's territorial claims by other states involves acceptance of its sovereign rights as the only legitimate source of power there.

The British state claims sovereignty over Great Britain, part of Ireland, part of Hong Kong (that part not leased from the Chinese), Gibraltar, and numerous small islands. Its claims are challenged in many places. Within Great Britain the challenges are mainly directed through recognised legitimate channels – as with Plaid Cymru and the Scottish Nationalist Party; outside Great Britain, military challenges are more common, as currently in Ireland and recently in the Falkland Islands. The latter examples illustrate the foundation of a state's sovereign power on its exclusive right to use coercive force within its territory. The British Army is the only legitimate force in Northern Ireland and the Falkland Islands, according to British sovereignty claims and the views of other states which respect those claims.

Within Great Britain, coercion is rare – although there is a police force to ensure law and order – and rule is by consensus. This is demonstrated explicitly by the use of popular elections to produce governments. After each election, the leader of the party that can control a majority in the House of Commons is invited to form a government by the Head of State, and the previous government is dissolved. Tenure of government is only temporary (a maximum of five years is allowed between elections), but while it is held it involves effective control of the state apparatus – the effective executive (Prime Minister and Cabinet), the legislature (Parliament), the administration (Whitehall), the military and the judiciary. The Head of State is little more than a figurehead, and sovereignty is expressed through the concept of the 'Crown in Parliament' (Rose, 1982) which, unlike some other countries such as the United States, does not involve a separation of powers. The elected government is expected to act within the framework of the unwritten British 'constitution', an evolving body of tradition which currently legitimises a liberal-democratic regime.

The major constraint on all British governments is not the constitution, however, but the country's position in the world-economy (Taylor, 1982). The British state is involved in political, military and, above all, economic interrelationships and competition with other states, which control its foreign, defence and trade policy. Such activity involves treaty arrangements with other states, such as those for the European Communities, the North Atlantic Treaty Organisation, and the General Agreement on Tarriffs and Trade, as well as the broader institutions of the United Nations Organisation and the Commonwealth.

Britain's political agenda is set by the constraints of the world-economy, and British governments attempt to reinforce or ameliorate world trends to the advantage of the British state. Thus the current recession in the world-economy has placed the restructuring of British capital at the centre of the political agenda; the various political parties offer different perspectives on solving the same problem – how to make Britain compete more effectively in a stagnant world-economy (Taylor, 1983).

Without a fundamental transformation of British society, 'making the British economy more efficient' must inevitably involve supporting British capital and, in particular, enabling the accumulation of capital to operate as smoothly and profitably as possible. This is the guiding principle of current Conservative party policy, with its preferences for monetary control and free trade, and also of the Labour party's recent conversion to protectionism. Each represents a different strategy for achieving the same goal.

In summary, then, the British state, like all others in the capitalist world-economy, fulfils two main roles – *legitimation* and *accumulation* (Johnston, 1982; Short, 1982b). The performance of these roles is summarised in Figure 2.1. This diagram is a purely heuristic device, since the different categories are interrelated – the internal political use of the 'Falklands Factor' by the Conservative govern-

Legitimation		Accumulation	
Internal	**External**	**Internal**	**External**
Elections – Law	Defence	Economic management	Currency
Policing and judiciary	International treaties	Social policies	Trade policies

Figure 2.1   The roles and functions of the state

ment in 1982 illustrates that. Nevertheless, Figure 2.1 is useful as a categorisation of the state's various functions, and it provides the framework for the remainder of this chapter.

The Political Geography of Legitimation

The core of the British state consists of the four 'home countries' which make up the United Kingdom of Great Britain and Northern Ireland. Demographically, politically, and economically this union is dominated by England. Hechter (1975) has interpreted the process of union as one of internal colonialism, with England as the core. The degree of colonial penetration varies among the three peripheral countries, however, and is reflected in the geography of legitimation.

Colonialism was most explicit in Ireland, so that today the main challenge to the legitimacy of the British state comes from the rump of that colonial activity, the territory of Northern Ireland created in 1922. An armed struggle there since 1969 has claimed more than 2,500 lives, continuing the problem of 'the Irish question' which has harried British politicians for more than a century. The armed struggle is complemented by electoral politics. A substantial minority of the Northern Ireland electorate has been prepared to vote against the British state (and the political parties of Great Britain have recognised this by declining to operate there). Until recently, the elected Nationalist candidates (who wish union with the Republic of Ireland, not Great Britain) have legitimised the British state by occupying their seats and accepting their roles within the state apparatus. (In the late 1970s, one Northern Ireland nationalist MP was partly responsible for keeping the Labour government in power.) But the election of candidates more directly aligned with the armed struggle has led to nationalist electoral participation while withholding recognition of the British parliamentary institutions of Westminster and Stormont.

The British response to this challenge to the legitimacy of the state was to take direct control of Ulster affairs and remove all power from the dissolved assembly at Stormont. (In 1982, Northern Ireland was allocated five more parliamentary seats at Westminster to compensate for the loss of Stormont and to give relative equality of representation with Scotland and Wales.) Northern Ireland has also been designated a separate security zone under the Prevention of Terrorism Act (1974) which allows the Home Secretary to interfere with individual freedom of movement within the United Kingdom through the power to ban UK citizens resident in Northern Ireland from entering Great Britain (i.e. the mainland).

Violent action against the British state has been sporadic and rare in the other two peripheral countries – Scotland and Wales. In the late 1960s–early 1970s nationalism flowered electorally in both countries, leading to a review of the unitary state as represented in the constitution (Rose, 1982; Madgwick and Rose, 1982). The resulting devolution proposals were put to a referendum, which showed that they were more popular in Scotland than in Wales but had insufficient support in either to become government policy. The nationalist vote declined in both countries at the 1979 general election, but devolution remains on the agenda of the largest political force in both, the Labour party.

The legitimacy of the British state has not been seriously threatened at a regional scale within England. The challenge to legitimacy within England has traditionally occurred in the inner cities, where low turnouts at elections indicate alienation from the state. This inner-city disillusionment has been compounded by the ethnic variety introduced through the immigration policies of the 1950s and 1960s. In the summer of 1981, a combination of general alienation plus the particular frustrations of the immigrants and their offspring stimulated widespread rioting in twenty-five towns and cities, plus nine locations within Greater London (Figure 2.2). The forces of law and order were challenged, even producing temporary 'no go' areas beyond the state's control – reminiscent of Northern Ireland in the mid-1970s. (A tacit policy of self-censorship by the media a year later meant that a similar riot in part of Liverpool went largely unreported and un-noted.)

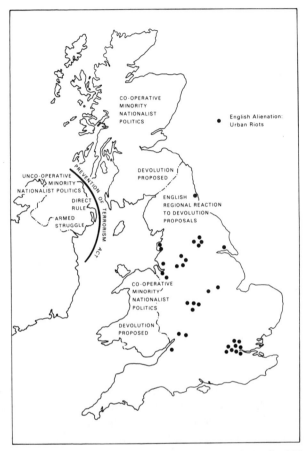

Figure 2.2   The political geography of legitimation in the United Kingdom

The Economic Geography of Accumulation

A major task of the state is to promote the success of capitalist enterprise domiciled within its territories; it must advance the cause of accumulation and create an environment within which investment will produce acceptable returns and enterprise will flourish. Any country is only as healthy as its economy, so the state must promote economic health.

State promotional activity occurs in three main ways. First, the state invests in means of increasing labour productivity. Second, it manages the economy to encourage accumulation, and operates a foreign policy conducive to the trading interests of its capitalists and investors. Third, it seeks to reduce the costs of labour by socialising some of the necessary expenses (on education, health and housing, for example); by doing this, it can also promote legitimation through arguments that it is 'subsidising' individual welfare and development.

A major example of investment in labour productivity is the provision of an adequate infrastructure of public services and utilities. Initially, the British state operated a legislative framework only for private investments in turnpike roads, railways, and canals, and it encouraged the provision of water, gas, electricity and other utilities, some by municipal enterprises. Increasingly, it has become directly involved in the provision of all of these. This infrastructure underpins the economic geography of Britain, and despite current attempts to 'privatise' some parts of it – parts of British Rail and British Telecom, for example – it is very unlikely that provision of roads, railways, electricity, gas, coal, water, etc. will be 'denationalised'. If it were, it is almost certain that private suppliers would concentrate on more profitable areas, with major consequences for the economic and social geography of the remoter and less densely peopled areas, where investment prospects would be dim (Johnston, 1982).

Beyond the basic infrastructure, the British state has become increasingly involved in particular industries. In general, its interests have been confined to investment in, and direct control over, particular industries and firms in the declining elements of British manufacturing. These are sectors in which growth was very rapid at earlier stages of the industrial development process. Demand for the products has now stabilised, and standard production methods have made British manufacturers uncompetitive against the output of low-wage employers elsewhere, both in southern and eastern Europe and in the Third World. Investment in these British industries has declined. The state has been encouraged to revive and protect them, however, because such industries are identified as crucial to the economy – even if they are not profitable (as with British Steel) – and because of the major job losses that would be incurred if decline continued. Thus, for example, the state has been advised by interest groups (including trades unions) to use import duties to protect industries such as textiles and to provide investment capital so that large firms such as BL can become competitive in the domestic and international markets. By promoting accumulation (profitable industries) it also assists legitimation (by providing employment opportunities).

This concentration on declining industries indicates a relatively conservative stance on the part of governments of both main parties in recent decades. Unlike France and other countries (and the current policies of the left in the British Labour party) relatively little has been done to stimulate growth industries. At the present time, the state has invested in microprocessor development, information technology, and bioengineering and it underwrites research in higher education, via the research councils; but the sums are small and do not compare with the amounts spent annually in the declining sectors: the British state prefers to protect existing employment than to generate new sources. There is a general belief – again widely held throughout the political parties – that stimulation (i.e. creating an environment that assumes profitability) is all that is required to ensure investment and growth in new industries, as in the promotion of cable television.

One consequence of this industrial policy, according to some commentators, is that it accentuates regional differentials in prosperity. The old declining industries are concentrated north of the Trent, and in Wales; the modern declining industries are in the West Midlands. The new, expanding industries are concentrated in the South East, in the towns of London's commuter belt and hinterland and along major routeways such as the M4 corridor; it is here that capital is accumulating fastest (Figure 2.3a). Industrial policy of the British state since the late 1950s has largely favoured encouraging growth wherever it wants to go. Regional policy is much weaker than it was, and despite lip-service and some past successes the British state is now not committed to national spatial planning. To those in power in London, national economic growth is the goal, wherever it may occur. (Sharpe, 1982, points out that this is true of the Labour party, despite its electoral strength in the declining areas.) Areas of severe economic and social distress (such as the inner cities) are offered some assistance, but the main task of promoting local employment opportunities has fallen to local governments, many of which are now active in seeking to protect and advance the job prospects of their constituents. The result is a

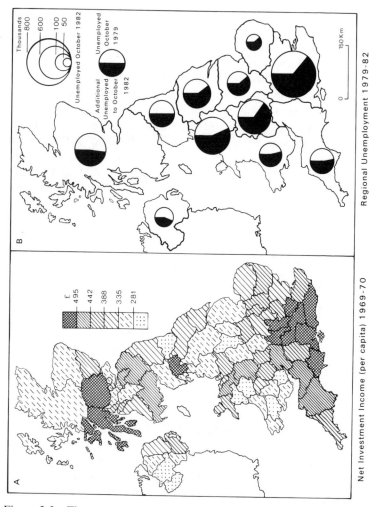

Figure 2.3   The economic geography of accumulation within the United Kingdom

(a) The accumulation of wealth as indicated by per capita incomes from non-employment sources (Schedule D). Source: R. J. Johnston and B. E. Coates, *Evidence to the Royal Commission on the Distribution of Income and Wealth*, HMSO, 1976.

(b) The changing geography of unemployment.

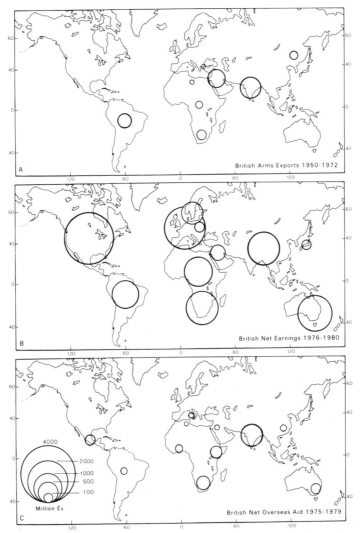

Figure 2.4   The economic geography of accumulation to the United
Kingdom

(a) British arms exports 1950–72 in $m (1968 constant). Source: Stockholm
International Peace Research Institute, *The Arms Trade with the Third World*,
Penguin, London, 1975, pp. 102–3.

(b) Net earnings of British companies (excluding oil) 1976–80, in £m. Source:
Business Monitor MA4, *Overseas Transactions, 1980*, HMSO.

(c) UK net overseas aid 1975–79, in £m. Source: Overseas Development
Administration, *British Aid Statistics 1975–1979*, HMSO.

plethora of unrelated local industrial strategies with no overall co-ordination. Territorial economic planning has become less important to the central state, as economic decline forces it to seek jobs at any price.

The second state function relating to accumulation, economic management, has little direct impact on the geography of the United Kingdom itself. Budgetary policies promoting growth are likely to favour certain areas over others, whereas deflationary policies with their attendant unemployment usually have a greater impact in some regions than in others (Figure 2.3b). But demand management, via control of the money supply, prices, and incomes, is largely aspatial. This is not the case with the promotion of British interests overseas, however.

A major function of the state for several centuries has been to promote and protect the interests of British capital overseas. The British Empire was built up as the political support for mercantile activity, and for the exploitation of overseas resources, labour and markets. The result was a geography of puppet states and a massive military presence throughout the world. With decolonisation, the puppet states have gone, but economic policies – including those of so-called 'aid' (Figure 2.4c) – have been created to maintain the dependent status of those new territories, and to tie them, as far as possible, to the British purse-string (McKinley and Little, 1978). At the same time, a variety of policies has been enacted to promote trade and other activities beneficial to British capital – as with the network of consulates and trade missions and the support for trade delegations (Figure 2.4b).

Foreign policy is very much tied up with the state's role in promoting accumulation. The protection of British interests influences the geography of diplomatic activity, and provides a rationale for opposing the introduction of competing interests – such as the perceived potential Communist takeovers of many African, American and Asian countries. The 'red menace' is countered with the defence of the 'free world' (Figure 2.4a) – whose freedoms include those of speech and assembly (sometimes) plus the exploitation of labour by capital (always). British entry to the EEC was advanced, in part, by the need for a united Europe to counter the military strength of the East.

The Geography of Government Activity

Britain was one of the pioneer 'welfare states'. It took over responsibility for the basic needs of its population – housing, health, education, a sufficient income to provide a subsistence diet – in order to mitigate the worst failures of the market economy, to ensure social cohesion in the face of increased protest, and to underwrite the reproduction of a satisfactory, and largely satisfied, workforce. In this, its twin functions of promoting economic success and maintaining the integrity of the nation coincide. They also provide the basis for conflict. The more that the state spends on its social policies, the more, it is argued, it harms its economic goals of promoting capitalist success: a delicate balance must be provided over the long term, while in the short term either economic or social goals may prevail.

It is the local governments, acting within the guidelines of central government policies and directives, that have been responsible for much of the detail of the welfare state. Provision of the educational system, apart from the universities, is undertaken by local authorities, for example, and is by far the largest element in their budgets. Services relating to the local environment, such as rubbish disposal and public health standards, to the protection of local property, and police and fire services, are also provided by local governments. But support for the unemployed and the poor, provision of the health service, and basic utilities such as water, electricity and gas, have been removed from local control in recent decades and taken over by *ad hoc*, non-elected bodies created by, and responsible to, the central state. In this way, the latter has obtained closer control over these areas of spending, which can be tuned in accordance with national economic management policies rather than local needs and demands.

The demands for the services that they provide put great pressure on local governments, who are unable to raise income apart from the unsatisfactory rating system. This system produces spatial inequalities, because areas in decline have lower property values to tax, and thus have less to spend, but greater demands. To correct these inequalities, and also to supplement the local tax base, the central state now make substantial grants to local governments (about 50–60 per cent of the latter's entire expenditure). This gives the central body substantial influence, if not control, over local policies, and enables it, by manipulation of the grant-allocation formula, to favour certain areas and groups over others (see Bennett in this volume). Thus the local government system, with its focus on provision of local welfare services, is put into conflict with the central state whose main concern is economic management. In a period of substantial economic decline, this conflict is heightened. It is exacerbated because the pressures on the central state mean that it has to determine spending priorities among its major functions. Successive governments have seen their principal task as the promotion of economic change, preparing an environment in which investment will increase, jobs will be created, and the economy will boom again. To do this, it is seen as necessary to cut social consumption expenditure of the welfare state, not only to allow more expenditure on investment but also to reduce the state's borrowing requirements, thereby (it is hoped) leading to reduced interest rates, and more borrowing and investment in private industry: hence cuts in education – especially those elements not perceived as relevant to industrial expansion – proposals to privatise parts of the health service, and plans to reduce the real value of unemployment payments.

One consequence of this shift in spending is a high level of unemployment, especially for the relatively unskilled and for those youths newly arriving on the labour market. This breeds alienation, and has been countered by a variety of training programmes operated by the Manpower Services Commission. Such alienation also provides a challenge to law and order, and has led to government support for the police services.

The Role of Elections

Recent British elections suggest growing disillusion with the parties that have governed the state, and indeed with the state itself. Turnout at general elections has declined since the Second World War, with only three-quarters of the electorate voting at the 1979 general election. The low turnout (32 per cent) at the European Parliament elections in 1979 indicates little enthusiasm for that potential route to economic recovery. Reasons for this electoral apathy include the progressive distancing of state from society, breeding a feeling among the population that voting is largely irrelevant. The vote is not seen as an instrument of change (unlike, for example, 1945); the SDP–Liberal Alliance claims that it can be once again, but a centrist coalition, should it come about, will produce the required political stability by making probability of significant change via electoral democracy even more remote.

Elections are not totally irrelevant, however, and certainly not to an understanding of the regional geography of government activity. They provide the passports to power, nationally and locally. Once an election has been won, it is a major task of incumbent governments to ensure that they are returned again at the next election. Some of the policies undertaken to this end may have spatial components – either intentionally or as unintentional consequences. An example of the latter was the tax policy introduced by the Conservative Chancellor of the Exchequer, Sir Geoffrey Howe, in his 1979 budget. In this, he cut income taxes, especially at the higher levels, and increased Value Added Tax. As the former is the more progressive of the two taxes, the result was a redistribution of real income towards the more affluent. And because the affluent are concentrated in the south, this meant a greater per capita input to the economies of some regions than others: estimates (Johnston, 1979b) suggest the following levels of increase in per capita annual spending power:

West Midlands	£30.67	Wales	£21.73
East Anglia	£29.14	Scotland	£21.47
South East	£28.84	North West	£21.41
East Midlands	£27.55	North	£20.20
South West	£27.15	N. Ireland	£17.17
Yorkshire	£25.36		

Intended spatial components to policies come about because incumbent governments seek to 'buy' votes in crucial constituencies. This is particularly apparent at by-elections when a government may make concessions to local interests – as with the promise of the Humber Bridge at a 1976 by-election in Hull. More generally, it comes about because of the geography of party support (Johnston, 1979a).

In terms of support for the two main political parties, Great Britain is a polarised island: the Labour party has traditionally been strongest in the urban-industrial areas of Scotland, Wales and northern England, plus inner-city areas further south (notably in

London); by contrast, the Conservative party has drawn most of its support from southern England, especially the rural areas, the suburbs, and the prosperous small towns. Since the 1950s this polarisation has been accentuated, more so in the distribution of parliamentary representation than of votes (Figure 2.5; Taylor, 1979); Labour won twenty-nine fewer seats in 1979 than in 1955 in the south and midlands, but sixteen more in the north of England.

Government policies reflect this spatial polarisation. With its electoral base in the declining industrial regions, Labour has pursued more active policies of regional development and spatial

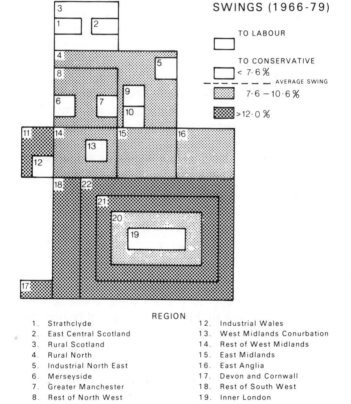

REGION

1.	Strathclyde	12.	Industrial Wales
2.	East Central Scotland	13.	West Midlands Conurbation
3.	Rural Scotland	14.	Rest of West Midlands
4.	Rural North	15.	East Midlands
5.	Industrial North East	16.	East Anglia
6.	Merseyside	17.	Devon and Cornwall
7.	Greater Manchester	18.	Rest of South West
8.	Rest of North West	19.	Inner London
9.	West Yorkshire	20.	Outer London
10.	South Yorkshire	21.	Outer Metropolitan Area
11.	Rural Wales	22.	Outer South East

Figure 2.5   The geography of voting

Source: P. J. Taylor, *Area*, 11, 1979, p. 291.

planning than have Conservative governments (see Sharpe, 1982, on their effectiveness). The Conservatives have limited their expenditure on regional policy and have restricted the area eligible for regional aid, preferring to stimulate growth in the modern, high-technology industries of the towns in southern England, such as those along the M4 corridors.

All governments favour their electoral heartlands, so the greater economic polarisation between south and north in Britain is reflected in voting patterns and government policies. Key areas, those that appear to hold the balance of power, are the ones most likely to benefit from such policies. (Labour will tend to the north and Conservatives the south; intense Conservative interest in northern problems is only likely when these threaten the cohesion and legitimation of the state as a whole, as with the response to riots in Toxteth in 1981.) Increasingly it seems that the West Midlands will be such a key area, as a consequence of the rapid decline of the once-buoyant car industry. Support for BL is just one element of the growing concern of Conservative politicians: as expressed by a Labour MP – 'What is it that the West Midlands has got that Manchester has not? . . . an abundance not of jobs but marginal parliamentary seats' (Gerald Kaufman, *The Times*, 7 February 1983).

New Geographies of Armageddon

The political debate with potentially the greatest relevance to the geography of modern Britain concerns that country's role as a forward base in NATO's nuclear strategy. The large-scale damage that a nuclear attack would inflict on Great Britain has forced the Home Office to devise contingency plans, comparable to those designed previously to cope with the consequences of an armed invasion. Given the likely breakdown in communications following a nuclear attack, a form of devolution will become operational, comprising twenty-one regions each with its bunker headquarters. With large-scale disruptions these would, in effect, become new sovereign territories, with 'capital cities' as indicated on Figure 2.6a.

This devolution proposal could reflect a relatively optimistic view of the likely impact of a nuclear attack, as suggested by a recent computer simulation that estimates 43 million deaths resulting

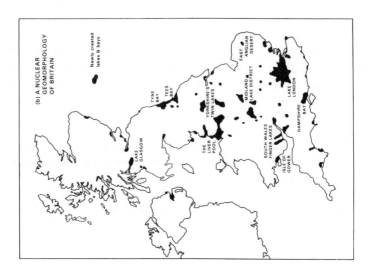

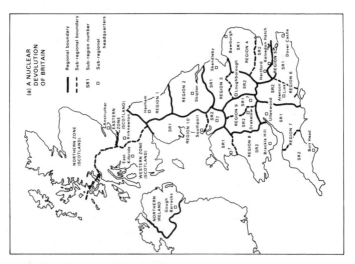

Figure 2.6 New geographies of Armageddon

(a) Regions and subregions to be used following a nuclear attack. Source: *New Statesman*, 2 October 1981.

(b) A post-nuclear geomorphology of Britain.

from a typical Soviet strike (Openshaw and Stedman, 1982). Most of these deaths would occur in the densely peopled areas, which contain many of the Home Office's regional centres (Figure 2.6a). The survivors would be concentrated in what are currently the remoter regions. In post-nuclear Britain, 'Main Street' is likely to be the Caledonian Canal connecting Fort William and Inverness, two of the largest surviving towns. Other 'major' population concentrations would probably be in North Wales and the far south-west of England.

Following Bunge (1982), and using Openshaw and Stedman's (1982) maps, we have produced a map of the post-nuclear geomorphology of the United Kingdom (Figure 2.6b). Disruption of waterways would produce widespread flooding and several major new hydrological features. Lake London will be Britain's finest 'natural' harbour, but will unfortunately be far from the major population concentrations. Similarly, the Liver Pool will have removed the inconveniences of the present Manchester Ship Canal, just when demand for movement there will have sharply declined. Possibly, recreational planners in the future will identify major development potential for Lake Glasgow, because of its proximity to the population centres of the Scottish Highlands.

Conclusions

The state is a critical element in a capitalist society, involved in promoting accumulation and legitimation. It is responsible for economic management programmes, political support for overseas economic activity, social programmes, social solidarity and national cohesion, defence of sovereignty, and maintenance of internal law and order. Much of this activity is geographical in its composition and consequences.

To understand the political geography of the world, one must appreciate the nature of the state. Similarly, to appreciate economic and social geographies one must appreciate the constraints and enabling factors that govern – but in no way determine – state activity. This chapter has sketched an outline of such understanding.

3
Industrial Location and Regional Development

David Keeble

Since the mid-1960s there seem to have been occurring simultane-
ously in Britain two very important economic trends. The first is
national manufacturing decline, or 'de-industrialisation' as it is
sometimes called, which is linked to high and rising unemployment.
Thus in the seventeen years to 1982, Britain's manufacturing sector
shed no less than 2.74 million workers, a staggering decline of 33
per cent, while industrial output grew only slightly and indeed
declined in the late 1970s. The collapse of British manufacturing
industry after 1979, more severe even than that of the dreadful
slump of the 1930s, reflected acute and intensifying world recession, continuing low investment, and declining international com-
petitiveness, all in the context of very severe financial pressures on
industry from the monetarist policies of a Conservative government
preoccupied with reducing inflation rather than unemployment.
Despite a big increase in government and private sector service
industry jobs (up in total by 1.91 million, or 17 per cent), national
unemployment therefore rose steeply and inexorably, to over 3
million workers or 13 per cent of Britain's total workforce by the
end of 1982 (see Figure 3.1). By that year, only 27.4 per cent of
Britain's employed workers were still working in manufacturing
(37.1 per cent in 1965), compared with 62.8 per cent in services
(only 48.8 per cent in 1965).

Geographically, however, manufacturing decline and unemployment growth have not been distributed evenly across the
country, reflecting a second general tendency, at least until the later
1970s, towards regional economic *convergence*. By the 1980s, the
regional distribution of both manufacturing and service industry
was considerably more even than it had been in 1965, with

previously big industrial regions such as the South East, North West and West Midlands declining especially rapidly relative to small rural or peripheral regions such as East Anglia, the South West, Wales and Northern England. Thus the share of national manufacturing employment in the first three big regions, which are of course located along the traditional London–Lancashire industrial axis of Britain, fell from 57.5 to only 54.5 per cent by 1982, while that of the four small rural or peripheral regions grew, from 16.2 to 19.1 per cent. For service industry – banking and insurance, transport, education, health, and so on – a somewhat similar relative shift occurred, with the South East growing more slowly (19 per cent over the period 1965–82) than any other region except the North West. In this case, the fastest-growing regions were East Anglia (40 per cent), the East Midlands (34 per cent) and the South

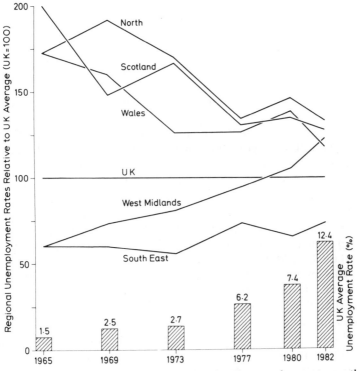

Figure 3.1   Regional convergence and national unemployment growth, 1965–82

West (25 per cent). Service job growth in the assisted regions (Wales, Scotland, etc.) has been mainly in public sector services, for welfare reasons.

Associated with these regional employment shifts, broad convergence has also occurred in regional rates of unemployment, female employment, population migration, and earnings (Keeble, 1977, 1980a). The relative improvement of regional unemployment rates in the assisted regions of Wales, Northern England and Scotland up to 1977 is clearly indicated by the accompanying graph (Figure 3.1), as is the West Midlands' steady deterioration throughout the period. Female employment (or activity) rates also rose much faster in Scotland, Northern England and Northern Ireland than in the country as a whole, because of a relative growth there of female-employing manufacturing and government services (Cambridge Economic Policy Group, 1980). By 1980, regional earnings per worker had also converged considerably, ranging between a Northern Ireland minimum for men of £114 per week (91 per cent of the UK average) and a South East maximum of £135 (108 per cent), the differences chiefly reflecting a greater absolute concentration of higher-paid jobs in the South East, rather than much higher earnings for similar jobs. Nearly all other regions fell between 95 and 100 per cent of the national average, with Scotland, a classic high-unemployment assisted region, actually having the second highest earnings level in the country after the South East. Lastly, regional migration estimates reveal a striking shift between the mid-1960s and late-1970s from net in- to net out-migration for the South East and West Midlands, but from net out- to net in-migration for Wales. Though net out-migration from Scotland and Northern England continued, the rate of loss fell, in the former case quite sharply. In the 1970s, the only gainers from net migration, in addition to Wales, were East Anglia, the South West and the East Midlands.

This broad picture of regional economic convergence, with big traditionally prosperous industrial regions such as the South East, West Midlands and the North West losing ground relatively to both problem peripheral regions such as Wales and Northern England and rural regions such as East Anglia and the South West, should however be qualified in at least two important ways. First, some geographers argue that relative regional employment gains by peripheral and rural regions during the 1960s and 1970s may well have masked an intensification of regional imbalances in the *quality* rather than number of jobs available to people in these regions (Massey, 1979). In particular, they suggest that the growth of big multi-plant companies has enabled such firms to hive off mass-production of standardised goods – washing machines, drugs, jeans – to regions where low-skill, low-wage and un-unionised female labour is readily available, while concentrating high-level, well-paid jobs in headquarters functions and specialised research-and-development units in the South East core. Certainly one recent study (Goddard and Smith, 1978) has shown that between 1972 and 1977 the South East *increased* further its already massive share of the headquarters offices – and presumably associated jobs – of the United Kingdom's top 1,000 companies (measured by turnover), from 58.6 to 62.2 per cent, to the detriment of the rest of the country.

The second qualification concerning regional convergence is that, as Table 3.1 shows, since about 1978 convergence appears to have

Table 3.1   Recession and regional manufacturing employment trends, 1978–82

	Manufacturing employment 1978 Change 1978–82				Manufacturing employment 1978 Change 1978–82		
	'000	'000	%		'000	'000	%
East Anglia	201	−28	−13.9	North West	999	−230	−23.0
South East	1862	−283	−15.2	North	418	−96	−23.0
Greater London	770	−146	−19.0	Scotland	604	−141	−23.3
Rest of S East	1092	−137	−12.6	Yorks–Humber	707	−169	−23.9
South West	427	−67	−15.7	West Midlands	989	−260	−26.3
East Midlands	599	−101	−16.9	Wales	312	−89	−28.5

been replaced by divergence, at least in terms of regional trends in manufacturing employment. Thus while manufacturing jobs in the peripheral assisted regions of Wales, Northern England and Scotland declined faster than in Britain as a whole (national average 20.6 per cent), manufacturing industry in the South East and its three adjacent regions of East Anglia, the East Midlands and the South West recorded slower rates of decline, with the 'best' performance of all British regions being in the South East outside London. Divergence is also apparent between 1977 and 1980 on the unemployment graph (Figure 3.1), as deepening manufacturing depression hit the assisted regions, with their specialisation in manufacturing industry, earlier and more severely than the South East, with its contrasting specialisation in service industry. After 1980, however, the spreading of the recession to all parts of the UK economy, including services, was no doubt an important factor in the resumption of regional unemployment rate convergence, albeit with bigger absolute unemployment rate differences (South East 9.0 per cent, Wales 15.9 per cent, North 16.5 per cent, in 1982) than at any time since the 1930s (Martin, 1982). Of special note is the collapse since 1970 of the West Midlands economy, with its overspecialisation in motor vehicles and mechanical engineering. This collapse is starkly illustrated by a rate of manufacturing job loss 1978–82 second only to Wales (Table 3.1), and by an accelerating rise in the West Midlands unemployment rate (Figure 3.1) to a 1982 level actually *above* that of Scotland, one of Britain's classic high-unemployment regions.

The reversal of previous core–periphery convergence in manu-facturing employment after 1978 is probably partly due to excep-tional decline in the once-traditional staple industries of the peripheral regions, such as iron and steel, textiles, and heavy engineering. Between 1977 and 1983, for example, British Steel was forced to cut its workforce by no less than 120,000 employees – a staggering 56 per cent job loss. Since 1970, the peripheral regions have witnessed the wholesale closure of such steelworks as Consett, Hartlepool, Workington, Irlam, Shotton, Ebbw Vale and Cardiff, together with Corby in the East Midlands. But assisted region manufacturing decline clearly also reflects the closure of branch factories of firms from the South East and West Midlands, previously attracted there by government regional policy grants (Henderson, 1980), in the face of severe national and international economic recession. Conversely, the relatively better performance of the South East outside London, East Anglia and the South West undoubtedly partly reflects the birth and growth here rather than elsewhere of entirely new industries and firms engaged in electron-ics, computers and other research-oriented, 'high-technology' activities.

These points concerning recent regional differences in rates of manufacturing employment decline touch on the general question of how to explain the long-run shifts in regional location of industry and jobs which have been occurring in Britain over the last thirty or so years. Fortunately, considerable light has been thrown on just this question by recent research, notably that by Fothergill and Gudgin (1982). The latter argue forcefully that changes in overall regional employment are basically a response to changes in the regional level of primary (mining, agriculture) and manufacturing employment, since the great bulk of *service* employment serves local markets and population and is dependent on income brought into the region by its primary and manufacturing industries (see Keeble, 1976, p. 201). Only perhaps in the case of London and the South East do truly national – and international – services (finance, banking, insurance, etc.; Keeble, 1980a, p. 102) form part of the regional economic base, an exception that helps to explain the continuing relative prosperity of the South East despite its manufacturing decline. Since primary industries do not exhibit major regional differences in employment (except for Wales and the North with coalmining, and East Anglia with agriculture), it is the marked differences in regional *manufacturing* employment change, so Fothergill and Gudgin argue, that really matter in explaining overall trends in regional employment.

Given this viewpoint, what factors explain the striking recent regional manufacturing shifts noted earlier? The two authors present considerable evidence in favour of their thesis that these shifts are a response to three structural factors, plus the impact of government regional policy. The first and most obvious structural factor is the effect of *inherited regional industrial specialisation*, given different national rates of employment change for different industries because of differences in demand for their products and degree of international competition. In the past, regional specialisation on particular industries has been important in explaining manufacturing decline and growth: steel, shipbuilding or textiles help explain decline in Scotland, Northern England and Wales, while specialisation on electronics or motor vehicles helps explain growth in the South East or West Midlands (Keeble, 1976, ch. 3). However, Fothergill and Gudgin show that by the 1970s this traditional structural influence was accounting for only a small part of regional manufacturing shifts, largely because with national de-industrialisation *most* manufacturing industries were declining nationally. Previous differences between growing and declining industries, and hence between growing and declining regions, had thus narrowed considerably.

The single most dominant factor in regional manufacturing employment shifts, therefore, is now a quite different structural consideration, namely variations in the *urban–rural composition* of different regions. Since the early 1960s, big urban areas – London, Birmingham, Glasgow, etc. – have been losing manufacturing employment at a remarkable rate (Keeble, 1978), whereas small

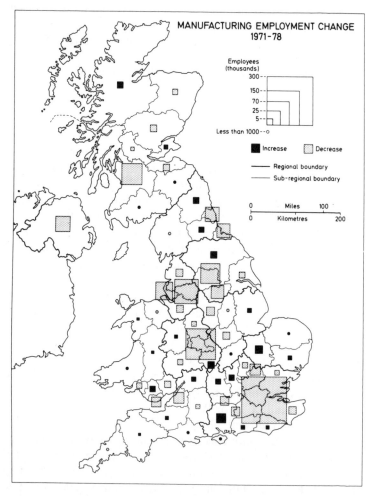

Figure 3.2   The geography of manufacturing employment change in the United Kingdom

towns and rural areas have been gaining jobs equally rapidly. Figure 3.2 reveals, in fact, that the leading counties of Britain in terms of manufacturing job gains in the 1970s were such non-industrial areas as the Highlands of Scotland, North Yorkshire, Cambridgeshire and Hampshire. Conversely, Greater London suffered the staggering loss of no less than 750,000 manufacturing jobs, or 55 per cent, over the twenty-year period to 1982. Indeed, there is a striking *continuum* (Figure 3.3) of manufacturing change spatially within the United Kingdom, with the greatest rates of decline concentrated in the most densely populated conurbations, less rapid but still considerable decline in big towns, slow decline in medium-sized towns, and manufacturing growth occurring only in really small towns and rural areas.

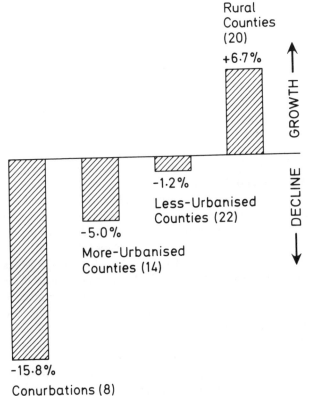

Figure 3.3   The urban–rural manufacturing shift in the United Kingdom: average rates of change in manufacturing employment, 1971–8

This remarkable *urban–rural manufacturing shift* (Keeble, 1980b) is explained by Fothergill and Gudgin as an inevitable consequence of rapid technological change and increasing capital–labour substitution in manufacturing since about 1960, in the context of the constrained locations and cramped sites which prevent firms from physically expanding their factories in urban areas.

The more urban and congested a settlement, the less room there is for new factory space, and the more labour has to be displaced when firms install new machinery. In rural areas and small towns, on the other hand, there is plenty of room for factory extensions, and capital investment can thus take place on a big enough scale to avoid making workers redundant. This process explains the striking differences in rates of employment change in *existing* firms in urban and rural locations, discovered by Fothergill and Gudgin. It is also a factor in the actual physical movement of growing urban firms to rural areas and small towns in search of space to expand. Migration of this kind is viewed by these authors as a secondary component in the urban–rural shift, along with higher rural birth-rates of entirely new firms, coming into existence for the first time.

However, there is also evidence that both migration and higher rural birth-rates may be influenced by a factor not regarded as important by Fothergill and Gudgin, namely the greater residential attractiveness of rural and small town locations to entrepreneurs, industrialists and key workers such as research scientists and engineers. This factor, together with the local availability of university-trained staff, would certainly seem to be important in the recent mushroom growth of new computer and electronics firms in a broad belt between Cambridge and Bristol (Hall, 1981). Between 1972 and 1982, the Cambridge area alone witnessed the establishment of over eighty entirely new high-technology firms in electronics, software, bio-engineering, lasers, etc, including such now-famous computer firms as Sinclair and Acorn. The choice of Winchester and Exeter, announced by Sinclair in 1982, as locations for additional new high-technology research units strikingly fits the residential preference hypothesis suggested above.

The dominance of the urban–rural shift as the single most important trend in industrial location in Britain also has major *regional* implications. For as Fothergill and Gudgin stress, regional manufacturing trends over the last thirty years chiefly reflect internal regional differences in urban–rural composition, the greatest regional declines inevitably occurring in regions that happen to be dominated by big congested conurbations (North West, West Midlands and South East), with regional growth only in regions that are largely rural (East Anglia, South West, Wales, and to some extent the North).

The third of the structural influences identified by Fothergill and Gudgin as affecting regional manufacturing trends in recent years is the *inherited size structure* of firms in different regions. According to the two authors, this is the dominant influence on regional rates of new-firm creation, in that small firms are in fact much more likely to spawn entrepreneurs who set up their own companies than are big firms. In the long run, this benefits regions such as the South East or East Midlands, relative to Scotland and Wales where big firms are important. Certainly recent research (Oakey, Thwaites and Nash, 1980) has revealed a significantly higher manufacturing innovation rate in the South East (144), East Anglia (188) and the South West (150) than in Scotland (88) or Wales (53), relative to the Great Britain average (100); this is apparently associated with a preponderance of smaller or medium-sized companies in the first three regions. The greater residential attractiveness of these areas for new-firm entrepreneurs is almost certainly also involved.

The last issue demanding attention is the impact of government regional policy on industrial location in Britain. Regional policy, operating through financial incentives (Regional Development Grants, and until 1977, the Regional Employment Premium) and factory building controls (Industrial Development Certificates), intensified considerably after 1960. As a result, many firms set up branch factories in the assisted regions, leading on one estimate to a policy-induced manufacturing growth there of 385,000 jobs between 1960 and 1976 (Moore, Rhodes and Tyler, 1977). While this is probably too large an estimate, since it ignores the differential regional impact of the urban–rural shift, there is little doubt that regional policy did have a substantial effect upon the location of manufacturing industry in Britain up to the mid-1970s: and manufacturing job growth in the peripheral regions in turn contributed to convergence in regional unemployment, migration and female activity rates. Since the mid-1970s, however, regional policy implementation has been much weaker, as national recession has reduced to a trickle the supply of growing mobile firms; incentives

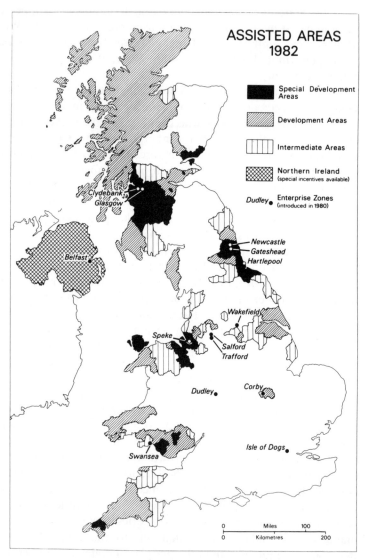

Figure 3.4 The assisted areas, 1982

have declined in value, and governments have ceased to operate IDC controls strictly. The last were in fact suspended (effectively abolished) in 1981, while the post-1979 Conservative government also cut severely both the level of Regional Development Grants (down from 20 to 15 per cent in Development Areas after 1979: see Keeble, 1980b) and the areas covered (down from 43 to 27 per cent of the working population by 1982). Areas still designated for regional policy assistance after August 1982 are shown in Figure 3.4.

The decline of regional policy is almost certainly one reason for the above-average manufacturing job losses experienced by the assisted regions of Wales, Northern England and Scotland since 1978 (Table 3.1). True, the early 1980s have witnessed new government initiatives to aid declining localities, in the form of the 'enterprise zones' established as part of inner-city rather than regional policy in derelict inner areas of cities such as Clydebank, Newcastle and Belfast. In these zones, industry enjoys considerable benefits, notably freedom from local government rate payments, tax allowances on new buildings, and reduced planning and other government controls. The first fourteen were designated in 1981 (Figure 3.4), while a second batch was designated in 1983. However, these zones are very small – generally only 200 to 500 acres – while most observers (Norcliffe and Hoare, 1982) are very doubtful as to their likely long-term effect on job creation and industrial regeneration. North Sea oil, another hoped-for catalyst of growth, has had only a limited and temporary impact on job creation in peripheral Britain (mainly in Scotland), while EEC regional policy aid, though potentially important, has had no significant effect because the British government insists on using it to offset the costs of its own regional expenditure. For Britain in general, and the assisted regions in particular, industrial and employment prospects for the 1980s seem more gloomy than at any time since the 1930s.

4
Changes in the Urban System

John Goddard

For a nation frequently chastised for its inertia, it is salutary to be reminded that Britain has just experienced two decades of almost unprecedented social and economic change. As the spectre of mass unemployment once again rears its head, it is important to realise that conditions are very different from those prevailing in the 1930s. In the post-war period, particularly since 1960, there has been a massive transfer of employment opportunities from manufacturing to services, from the private to the public sector, from manual to white-collar jobs, and from jobs for men to jobs for women. Notwithstanding these structural shifts there has also been an almost unabated rising trend in unemployment as the growth of employment opportunities has failed to keep pace with the growth in the supply of labour. In spite of this there has been an overall increase in material standards of living, reflected in such indicators as substantial increases in car and home ownership.

Changes in the structure of our towns and cities are an outward and visible sign of underlying social and economic trends. Without the benefit of a time-machine, a simple way of appreciating the scale of change today would be to take a train journey from Bristol to Newcastle and return by car, taking the motorway. The railway journey would pick out the centres of cities, basically the product of the industrial revolution, that are now showing numerous signs of their age. The motorway journey would reveal the scale of expansion on the periphery of towns in the form of space-extensive manufacturing, warehousing and hypermarket developments. It would also reveal the revival of growth in the market or county towns of England. Such a journey would emphasise that urban change is not just a feature of the largest cities but of the urban

52

system as a whole. If one could still catch a train, the similarities with the United States would be striking.

The Definition of Cities

All this can be appreciated from casual observations. However, the measurement of the true extent of the social and economic changes is more difficult. The chief problem is one of defining 'the town'. Our Victorian forefathers had a clear idea of what constituted towns and cities and embodied their ideas in Urban Districts and Municipal and County Boroughs which remained in use for administrative and statistical reporting purposes right up to 1974. The new set of Districts introduced in 1974 showed more sympathy for administrative convenience and political expediency than for local geography. So in order to provide an adequate delineation of towns and cities, particularly one that recognises the sphere of influence of a place beyond the edge of its built-up area, it is necessary to construct special definitions.

American statistical agencies have been more concerned with defining urban areas than their British counterparts. They have long recognised Standard Metropolitan Statistical Areas which are used by the US Census and other federal agencies. In Britain a number of attempts have been made by academic geographers to define approximate equivalents. The first was by Hall *et al.* (1973) using data from the 1961 Census of Population. These areas were referred to as Standard Metropolitan Labour Areas (SMLAs). Each SMLA consisted of an urban core with 20,000 or more jobs and a metropolitan ring from which more than 15 per cent of the working population commuted to the core. To be recognised as an SMLA the core plus its ring required a combined population of 50,000. In addition, an outer metropolitan ring was defined from which more workers commuted to the particular urban core than to any other core. As a very crude approximation the urban core could be equated with the pre-1914 built-up area, while the 15-per-cent commuting hinterland included the inter-war suburbs and some areas beyond.

These definitions were updated in 1971 by Spence (1982) and others, and 126 SMLAs covering nearly 80 per cent of the British

population were identified. More recently a fundamental reappraisal of the definition has been undertaken by Coombes *et al.*
(1982). This last approach involved the inclusion of a criterion of
retail provision in the identification of centres, but retained the
15-per-cent commuting criterion for the identification of hinterlands around these centres. There is also a more rigorous examination of the commuter boundaries between competing potential
centres in relation to the minimum population size threshold of
50,000 and the degree of 'self-containment' measured in terms of
the proportion of the population both living and working in the
area. This examination encompassed the whole country, so that no
residual or unclassified areas were left as was the case with the
SMLAs. Regions that do not reach the minimum population
threshold of 50,000 but which nevertheless qualify on all other
grounds are referred to as 'rural areas'.

There were 228 'Functional Regions' identified for use with the
1981 Census. As many of the larger cities are surrounded by a
number of subordinate towns (i.e. towns with a significant out-flow
of commuters to the larger city), 20 'Metropolitan Regions' can be
identified which include 93 sub-dominant centres contained within
their higher level sphere of influence. The remaining 115 towns
with no subordinate centres can be classified as 'Free Standing'.

Intra Urban Trends

Tables 4.1 and 4.2 for the period up until 1974 and 1971
respectively show that the dominant pattern has been one of first
population then employment de-centralisation from employment
cores to metropolitan rings and later outer rings. During the 1950s,
population was already declining in the cores of the nation's largest
cities and growing most rapidly in the metropolitan rings; however,
jobs continued to increase in the cores. Then, during the 1960s, half
a million jobs were lost in the urban cores, with metropolitan rings
gaining nearly three-quarters of a million workplaces. People and
jobs also moved into areas only weakly linked to the urban centres.
Indeed by 1974 the unclassified or rural areas were experiencing a
decennial rate of population increase of 4.1 per cent, a phenomenon
that would appear to be unrelated to growth of urban-based
employment opportunities. Actual figures for the ten years up to

Table 4.1   Population change, Great Britain, 1951–74

	1951–61 Million cities %	Rest %	1961–71 Million cities %	Rest %	1971–74* Million cities %	Rest %	% GB popn. 1971
Urban cores	−3.7	6.9	−9.0	3.5	−10.0	0.3	47.4
Metropolitan rings	10.2	16.4	13.1	21.0	1.8	10.0	31.9
Outer metropolitan rings	7.2	2.2	14.7	8.6	7.0	8.3	16.4
Unclassified areas	−0.9		−1.4		+4.8		4.3

* Ten year rate

Table 4.2   Employment change, by place of work, Great Britain, 1951–71

	Million cities %	Rest %	Million cities %	Rest %	% GB Emp. 1971
Urban cores	3.7	12.3	−9.1	8.4	58.6
Metropolitan rings	11.0	9.0	20.7	21.9	22.9
Outer metropolitan rings	6.7	−3.3	14.0	21.2	14.5
Unclassified areas	−5.5		−0.7		4.1

1981 (Table 4.3), although for a different definition of rural areas, reveals an overall rate of population growth outside urban Britain of 8.8 per cent. At the same time, population continued to decline in the urban cores, with this decline extending from the larger cities to characterise urban Britain as a whole.

The pattern of population and job de-centralisation has been highly differentiated. The outward movement of population has been spearheaded by the higher socio-economic groups but with

Table 4.3   Population change 1971–81, functional regions

	% Change	
	Million cities	Rest
Urban cores	−10.9	−9.0
Metropolitan rings	8.1	13.1
Outer metropolitan rings	17.0	14.7
Rural areas	8.8	

many of their managerial jobs remaining behind in the city centre. It has been blue-collar manual jobs that have declined most rapidly in the urban cores and at a higher rate than the decline of population in lower socio-economic groups. According to one estimate, the proportion of inner-city jobs taken by inner-city residents fell on average from 80 per cent to 70 per cent between 1951 and 1976.

Table 4.4   Population, employment and net commuting: conurbation inner cities 1951–76 (1951 = 100)

	1951	1961	1971	1976
Population of working age	100	95	79	72
Employment	100	101	86	79
Net inward commuting	100	123	126	128
Employment less net commuting	100	96	76	67

Source: *Cambridge Economic Policy Review*, vol. 8, no. 2, 1982.

These trends can be summarised in Table 4.4 which shows that in the inner cities of six conurbations (which do not correspond to the urban cores of the functional regions) the decline of jobs not filled by commuters exceeded the decline of working-age population. The consequence of these trends has been a rising level of unemployment in the urban cores, well above the rate of increase in unemployment found elsewhere in urban Britain (Table 4.5). According to the Census definition of unemployment (which relates to the areas where people live), unemployment rates in 1981 were significantly higher in urban cores and had grown more rapidly there since 1971 than in any other zone.

How can these changes be interpreted? The dispersal of popula-

Table 4.5   Residential unemployment rates: functional regions, 1971–81

	% 1971	% 1981	Acceleration rate*
Cores	5.3	10.9	104
Rings	4.3	7.9	81
Outer areas	4.4	7.8	79
Rural areas	5.5	8.8	61
Total	5.1	9.8	94

* ((1981% − 1971%) ÷ 1971%) × 100

tion from cities is long-established, representing a deep-seated desire for single-family living in semi-rural surroundings. During the 1930s the development of extensive suburbs was made possible by mass public transport. Urban containment policies in the 1950s succeeded in diverting suburbanisation to locations beyond the green belt, while employment, especially in the expanding white-collar occupations, continued to grow in the city centres. Other public policies, particularly comprehensive renewal of the nineteenth-century stock of housing in the urban core and the development of new and expanded towns, further reinforced the natural tendency of population dispersal in the 1960s, with 1,100,000 people migrating from the cores to the rings of British cities between 1966 and 1971.

The pattern of employment change is more complex. The growth of population in metropolitan rings has in time led to a growth in service activities including shops, schools and health care. Most of this has been in the form of female part-time employment. Thus the proportion of women of working age in, or seeking, employment increased more rapidly in the metropolitan rings than anywhere else in Britain between 1961 and 1971. In contrast, employment losses in the urban cores were characteristically male jobs in the manu-facturing industry. This decline affected all sectors of industry and cannot be attributed to the concentration in urban cores of the least-successful sectors.

Manufacturing employment decline in the largest cities has been principally due to the closure of factories and the contraction of those that have survived, rather than to their migration to the suburbs and beyond. The inner parts of cities with their cramped factory sites no longer provide a good environment for modern manufacturing industry. Multi-storey buildings are unsuited for automated production lines; faced with the difficulties of expanding on site, many small entrepreneurs have foregone investment in new products and production processes and have eventually gone out of business as a result. On the other hand, some large companies have transferred production to other locations in Britain and also abroad. Many of the founders of new enterprises have also long since left the inner areas in search of better residential conditions and have chosen to establish their businesses near to their homes.

Outside the manufacturing sector there have been major tech-nological changes which have directly reduced the demand for labour in urban cores and have also encouraged locational change. The changeover from manufactured town gas to natural gas has created a distribution industry which has inevitably followed the movement of population to metropolitan rings. The advent of containerisation has displaced jobs in city-centre ports and marshalling yards in favour of 'roll-on/roll-off' facilities at coastal locations. The East End of London has thus been laid waste by the successive closure of the London Docks, while Liverpool, lacking an indigenous manufacturing base, has been even more dramatically affected. The inner parts of large cities have also traditionally been the focus for postal services and telecommunications; the former has lost out to the latter in terms of its share of the nation's message services, while within telecommunications electronic technology has substantially reduced labour requirements. Finally, within retailing, supermarkets and hypermarkets are far less labour-demanding than space-demanding.

The only sectors where employment has grown dramatically in the urban cores are insurance, banking and finance, and headquarters office functions. The mushrooming of office blocks in city centres during the 1960s bore testimony to this trend. Many of these simply replaced older premises at lower densities of occupation. But even in the office sector dispersal has been occurring. In the case of London the blandishment of a rural idyll by the late Location of Offices Bureau successfully lubricated a market where dispersal was already taking place. Again, developments in technology were an important factor, permitting the dispersal of routine work which could be controlled from a central location where senior staff remained in order to keep in face-to-face contact with other businesses. Even in the office sector, automation is now beginning to reduce the need for clerical staff. Empty office blocks may therefore become a permanent feature of our city centres.

Inter Urban Trends

It would be wrong to assume that the patterns of decentralisation that have been described have been contained within the broadly defined Functional Regions. Even when their immediate commuting hinterlands are included the largest cities have experienced absolute population decline. Thus the London Functional Region, which extends almost to the South coast, lost 740,000 people between 1971 and 1981; the major provincial centres (Birmingham, Manchester, Liverpool, Glasgow and Newcastle) together lost 517,000.

Much of this dispersal has ended up in the sub-dominant towns and cities in the broader Metropolitan hinterlands – such places as Reading, Chelmsford and Crawley around London, Tamworth and Stratford-on-Avon around Birmingham, Chester and Southport around Liverpool, Warrington and Buxton around Manchester and Durham around Newcastle. Because employment as well as population has grown in these towns they have become urban centres in their own right, with their own hinterlands but with a significant number of commuters still travelling to the centres of the Metropolitan Region. Nevertheless, in the case of the largest Metropolitan Regions, growth in these 'sub-dominant' cities has not offset the decline of the dominant centres, and the whole Metropolitan Region has revealed absolute population decline. This has not been the case in the smaller Metropolitan Regions like Edinburgh, Nottingham and Bristol where population growth in sub-dominant regions has far exceeded the decline of the dominant centre, or in the freestanding towns of urban Britain; indeed the latter group as a whole recorded a 5.8 per cent population growth over the period 1971–1981 (Table 4.6).

Those ten Free Standing Functional Regions with the highest absolute population growth between 1971 and 1981 are listed in

Table 4.6 Population change by type of functional region, 1971–81

	Absolute ('000)	% Change
London metropolitan region		
Dominant region	−740	−8.6
Sub-dominant regions	303	7.2
Provincial conurbation metropolitan regions		
Dominant region	−517	−8.3
Sub-dominant regions	116	2.1
Other metropolitan regions		
Dominant region	−58	−0.8
Sub-dominant regions	379	5.2
Freestanding regions	1,118	5.8

Table 4.7 Functional regions ranked by absolute population change, 1971–81

1	Milton Keynes	60,995
2	Norwich	57,580
3	Cambridge	50,447
4	Peterborough	47,732
5	Northampton	36,910
6	Bournemouth and Poole	36,401
7	Aberdeen	36,383
8	Inverness	34,959
9	St Austell	31,136
10	Luton and Dunstable	30,795

Table 4.7. The table demonstrates that the largest population growth has occurred in East Anglia, in oil-related areas in North East Scotland, and in retirement areas of the South West. Much of this growth occurred in relatively small settlements which did not cross the 50,000 population threshold in 1971 but which nevertheless were clearly identifiable centres with commuting hinterlands. The list of places with the ten highest relative population growth rates between 1971 and 1981 includes places like Huntingdon, Bury St Edmunds and Banbury as well as major centres like Northampton and Peterborough (Table 4.8). All these places now qualify for urban status on a 50,000 population criterion. While some of the centres have benefited from New and Expanded Town

Table 4.8 Functional regions ranked by relative population change, 1971–81

		% Change	1981 Population
1	Milton Keynes	60.8	161,335
2	Dingwall and Invergordon*	34.0	50,244
3	Thetford*	30.4	70,446
4	Huntingdon*	24.7	71,083
5	Peterborough	23.4	199,180
6	Telford	22.5	163,888
7	Northampton	18.0	241,908
8	Newmarket and Ely	18.0	98,940
9	Banbury	18.0	78,550
10	Bury St Edmunds	17.3	70,168

* Rural Areas (i.e. regions with population of less than 50,000 in 1971)

status, many represent the classic market towns of rural England. So, much of the growth that occurred during the 1970s took place in small settlements well away from the main urban centres.

While these processes of inter-urban redistribution of population have mainly operated within the major regions of Britain, they have also been superimposed on the long-established decline of peripheral regions in the northern part of the country and the growth of the South East core region. Nevertheless it is extremely important to examine changes at this scale in urban terms. Within the peripheral regions the bulk of employment losses have occurred within the largest cities. While regional policies encouraged the movement of manufacturing industry into these regions, this has chiefly benefited the smaller towns. Nevertheless, Table 4.9 reveals that private manufacturing employment has been declining more rapidly in the subordinate cities surrounding the provincial conurbations than in similar centres around London or elsewhere in urban Britain.

While manufacturing industry has been dispersing to peripheral regions and declining at well below the national average in freestanding towns, Table 4.9 also reveals that the expanding

Table 4.9   Employment change by functional region 1971–81 (% change)

	London metropolitan region		Provincial conurbation metropolitan regions		Rest of Britain
	Dominant	Sub-dominant	Dominant	Sub-dominant	
Private manufacturing industry	−25.2	−3.6	−15.0	−10.2	−3.4
Nationalised industry	−18.7	−24.0	−18.4	−18.0	−10.4
Transport and distribution	−7.6	13.0	−11.4	5.1	6.2
Construction	−8.8	8.0	−9.3	6.6	3.0
Consumer services	−24.8	−2.5	−13.6	−10.8	−5.2
Business services and finance	8.0	47.8	14.2	31.5	34.5
Public services and administration	8.8	18.8	19.5	21.1	18.2

business service sector has exhibited even greater variations in rates of employment change between types of urban area in different parts of the country. Here the distinction is principally between areas surrounding London, which recorded a 47.8 per cent increase in business services and finance between 1971 and 1978. This contrasts with a mere 14.2 per cent increase in the provincial conurbations. The growth of areas around London is partly attributable to dispersal from the capital, a process confined largely to the South East region because of the costs of maintaining contact with the City of London and its financial institutions. An equally important factor, however, is the national concentration of the headquarters functions of British companies in the South East. As more manufacturing industry in peripheral regions is controlled by companies in the South East, the importance of provincial cities as business service centres has declined.

To exemplify this point, it can be noted that nearly 80 per cent of manufacturing employment in the Northern Region is controlled from outside the region, compared with slightly more than 50 per cent fifteen years ago. Survey results reveal that 77 per cent of the business service needs of such non-locally owned firms are purchased outside the region. By way of contrast, the same proportion of service needs of locally controlled firms are provided within the region, mainly from Newcastle. So, notwithstanding its size, Newcastle is losing its functional status within the hierarchy of control of British industry. Similar conclusions apply to the other provincial capitals. In contrast, London, with 525 headquarters of the thousand largest UK companies in 1977, has maintained a dominant position. Significantly this number had increased by 105 over the previous five years chiefly as a result of the acquisition of companies based outside London. One significant consequence of this trend has been the contribution to a new division of Britain into a white-collar South and a blue-collar North, which cuts across the city size hierarchy, with small towns in its South East having a more significant representation of managerial elites than much larger cities in the North.

Conclusion

While lower levels of population and economic growth in the 1980s are likely to reduce the pace of change within and between cities, the consequences of the major shifts that have occurred in the recent past will have to be lived with for some considerable time into the future. For example, the dispersed pattern of living that has emerged around networks of smaller settlements will be expensive to sustain given high energy costs. In addition, small settlements depending on one or two employers may be particularly vulnerable. In the case of the larger cities, while the earlier decline of employment in urban cores lagged behind the fall of population, thus creating no serious problems of unemployment, the rate of job loss is now exceeding that of population. The wholesale 'de-industrialisation' of Britain that is currently under way is having its most serious impact on the large cities. Indeed, some might argue that the significant share of productive capacity still based in older cities has partially contributed to this de-industrialisation because of the constraints on efficiency imposed by an outworn location. The widespread introduction of new technology into service industries, coupled with public expenditure cuts, may also mean that previously important sources of job opportunities in these sectors may be foreclosed. The problem is therefore not simply one of the inner areas, but of the overall decline of the major cities that still dominate the British urban system.

5
The Geography of Public Finance

R. J. Bennett

Public finance and the patterns of government spending are major topics of debate in most Western countries at present. Monetarist theory vies with Keynesian and neo-Keynesian prescriptions for management of the economy; urban fiscal crises, popular demands for taxation cuts (such as the California Proposition 13 in 1978) and the increasing rigour of public expenditure control of both the Reagan and Thatcher administrations, are all provoking intense controversy.

Much of the current debate over public finance contains overriding geographical features. For example, the reform of the Rate Support Grant in Britain has severely modified the rate bills of different social groups, and has markedly shifted central subsidy of local services from cities towards suburbs and rural areas. On the one hand these changes affect the spatial patterns of the *burdens* or costs of the public economy through revenue-raising, taxation and tax-exporting. On the other hand these changes affect the spatial distribution of the *benefits* of public finance: expenditure, service qualities and in-kind transfers. The net balance of these two features is the central focus of the geography of public finance.

Three Focuses for the Geography of Public Finance

The central issue of public finance is the distributional question of how the 'national cake' is divided: how resources are allocated between industries, individuals, programmes and locations. In assessing these distributional consequences of public finance there are three main focuses for geographical concern: namely tapering, jurisdictional partitioning, and spillover.

Tapering

Tapering describes the commonly observed phenomenon that the access to the benefits from a public service diminish, or taper off, with distance from the point at which they are supplied: the familiar neighbourhood effect. This differential access affects travelled-for goods such as hospitals, schools and recreation facilities because the cost or time of travel increase with distance from the source of supply. Differential access also affects supplied goods, however, when a central distribution point rather than a fixed network is employed. For example, with police protection, the fire service and ambulance service, the quality of service benefits in general declines with distance from the point of supply. This distance decay of access or service quality allows the development of a geographical theory of public good provision as an extension of the Losch-Christaller central place theory. The Löschian theory is based on the two familiar concepts of the price funnel and the demand cone, shown in Figures 5.1 and 5.2.

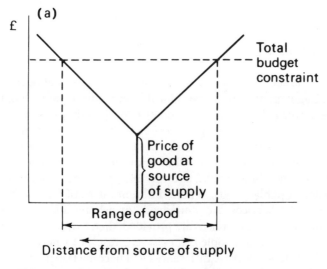

Figure 5.1   Lösch's concept of the price funnel of a good

[The total cost to the consumer of obtaining a given good is a combination of the over-the-counter price at the source of supply plus its transport costs to obtain it. When subject to a budget constraint this leads to the definition of the *range* of a public good]

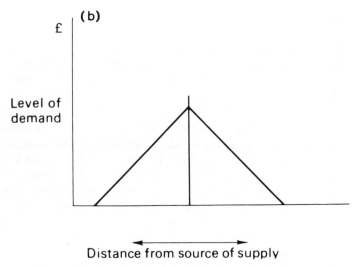

Figure 5.2   Losch's concept of the demand cone for a good

[Tapering of demand under the influence of transport costs resulting from price effects shown in Figure 5.1]

Jurisdictional partitioning

This is the second major focus for the geography of public finance. The fragmentation of geographical space into separate political units governed by semi-autonomous local authorities has been frequently ignored in geographical enquiries. Yet it has profound effects on the social distribution of public service benefits and costs. Each separate jurisdiction will have different financial resources, variable expenditure needs, and variable preferences for particular bundles of public goods. Where different mixes of local taxes and charges for services are employed, or where different levels, qualities or types of services are provided, then extreme differences in the treatment of people can exist as a result of where they live. The importance of these differences will become the greater where the number of local governments juxtaposed in a given area becomes the larger. Such differences are particularly important in the fragmented city governments (such as those characterising the United States), but also have great significance in the metropolitan counties and between the London boroughs in Britain. These jurisdictional differences become more significant if, as is usually the case, they correspond also with social, income or racial differences. In this case, poor people, disadvantaged groups, or ethnic minorities may coincide with poor local authorities, which are the least able to provide the services that are required. The result is often then a cycle or 'poverty trap' where higher taxes are required in the poorer local authorities to meet the higher expenditure needs of their more disadvantaged population. When this cycle has run full course it can result in massive city decay and in fiscal crises and even bankruptcies of the local government, as occurred in New York in 1975.

Spillover

Spillover is the third major focus of the geography of public finance. This describes the mismatching of the area that bears the cost of providing public services and the area that receives the benefit. Spillover is a direct result of jurisdictional partitioning. Benefit spillover occurs when public services are used by groups living outside the local authority providing the service. This so-called 'free-rider' problem is often claimed to characterise the use of central city services by suburban dwellers: the 'suburban exploitation of the central city' hypothesis. However, the evidence in support of this hypothesis is equivocal (see Bennett, 1980). Cost spillovers (or spillins) occur when people in one area pay towards the costs of services in another without receiving comparable benefit. An important example of this spillover is tax-exporting where the taxes levied in one area are shifted to a significant extent to other areas. For example, taxes on fossil fuels which are sold largely to other areas in the Northern United States allow over 30 per cent of the tax burden of Louisiana and Texas to be exported.

The Relation of Public Finance to Aggregate Social and Economic Change

The finance of the state is in part an artefact and in part a cause of social and economic change, and spatial relocation. Hence, any understanding of the relation of public finance to aggregate economic and social change must be well-grounded in the more general causes of change. For most preliminary purposes, this explanation can be approached from three points of view: quantitative and qualitative shifts in the spatial aspects of economies, and their relation to the organisation structure of public finance. Each aspect is discussed in turn below.

Quantitative change

This relates to the shift of population and economic growth in an economy. In most advanced Western countries this is now mainly the shift away from older industrial areas at two scales: urban and regional. At the urban scale, this presents a pattern of shift of major growth of both population and industry to the suburbs and to the satellites beyond the cities, sometimes termed counter-urbanisation. The adequacy of this statement has recently been questioned, since it lacks any real explanation of the forces generating change in metropolitan areas. Nevertheless, for our purposes in this chapter it is an adequate description of the reality for many cities.

At the regional scale, quantitative change in the location of the major growth stimuli in the economy is also occurring. In the most general terms this is again a shift from the older industrial areas to newer locations, often linked with demands for pleasanter environments or a smaller town and more rural location. Clearly this phenomenon is interlinked with that of counter-urbanisation, but at the regional scale it is an urban–rural shift of the major growth points of population and economic activity to locations that present either better growth prospects, less environmental problems, or other incentives to investment.

At both scales of change in growth stimuli two features must be distinguished: actual relocation and differential rates of growth. The extent to which counter-urbanisation, urban–rural shift and regional growth disparities result from actual relocations (i.e. migration of population or movement of industry) is probably fairly limited, although it is nevertheless important. In addition, a major cause of differences in rate of growth results from (i) the location of *new* industry in the outer metropolitan areas, (ii) the entry of people into the urban system to these areas as a first destination, and (iii) the location of the higher rates of population increase in the suburbs and outer metropolitan areas as a result of their demographic character.

Qualitative change

Interrelated with quantitative changes in the location of growth of economic activity and population, qualitative changes are also often occurring. In terms of relocation decisions, qualitative changes in population result from demographic and social filtering. It is the people in the relatively mobile age groups (approximately 18–30) with the more modern educational and technological skills who are those primarily able to move to the locations of new economic activity. Additionally, it is the individuals not in the lower socio-economic groups who find mobility easier, are more upwardly mobile and hence can match job mobility to spatial mobility, and have the purchasing power and personal economic orientations which make small town and 'rural' lifestyles both more attainable and desired.

As a result, the migrant groups in the population tend to be the relatively young, middle class and upwardly mobile. Left behind are the older, the poorer, and those with out-of-date skills. This induces an important qualitative shift in population characteristics.

The relocation of economic activity shows analogous tendencies. The mobile firms are those which have buoyant profits and growth prospects; indeed, it is often the need for new or expanded premises which precipitate a move outside of the older central cities. These cities often cannot provide for the larger space demands of the modern plant, and hence a green-field site at the edge of the city, or beyond, is essential.

The structure of public finance

The relocation of population and economic activity, or the shift of growth stimuli at urban and regional scales, would have little or no direct public finance consequences for cities if it was not for the fact that all Western countries operate a system of shared responsibility for public service between central and local levels. As a result, the responsibility of many services falls to the cities and these are usually financed, to some extent at least, by locally raised taxes and fees. In addition, inter-governmental aid in the form of grants and shared revenues is normally transferred from central or Federal and State levels to the local level of the city.

In determining the impact of aggregate forces of social and economic change, therefore, we must question the manner of organisation of expenditure, revenues and inter-governmental aid; and their interrelation with the organisation of the jurisdictional structure of space (i.e. the fragmentation of space into local government units). The quantitative and qualitative changes in population and economic activity outlined above have major impact on expenditure where responsibility for local service provision is high (as it is in the cities of most countries, certainly in the United States, United Kingdom, and Germany), where these expenditures relate heavily to fixed costs which do not reduce with decline, and where expenditures are strongly related to the income levels of the local population such that the relatively higher concentrations of the poor in declining areas lead to relatively higher per capita needs to provide services. On the revenue side, decline has more major impact the higher is the local area's responsibility for raising its own revenue.

Without the impact of inter-governmental aid, the relatively high concentrations of high-need categories for public services of old and poor people, and declining industry, in the problem regions and in central and declining cities, place disproportionately high revenue burdens on residents of these areas. In contrast, the relatively high concentrations of low-need, high-income categories of people and the rapidly growing economic base in the suburbs and satellites, place disproportionately light revenue burdens on the residents in the growing areas. This problem will be heightened by social filtering and the mobility of the higher-income groups. The more mobile industry may also relocate which may further stimulate other industries to move.

This has led some commentators to propose a model of 'financial crisis' which suggests two extreme cases. On the one hand, the growing areas have high income, buoyant tax base and relatively low expenditure need. This results in low and decreasing tax rates and hence lower total local tax burdens. On the other hand, the declining areas have low income, declining tax base and expenditure need which is increasing in relative (per capita) terms. This in turn results in high and increasing tax rates and hence higher total local tax burdens. For the declining areas, therefore, there is an increasing *needs-resources gap* and it is this which stimulates the use of the term 'financial crisis'. In contrast, the growing areas have expanding tax bases and a needs-resource surplus which allows them to enjoy the benefits of economic growth. Most important, however, quantitative and qualitative changes in the location of people and economic activity can in extreme cases set off a cumulative process of decline. Certainly, although not a cause of these changes, the impact of public finance is to work in the same direction as, and hence to reinforce, cumulative growth and decline. These problems will also become the more heightened the greater is the degree of fragmentation of local government in terms of the areal boundaries of local government power. This problem is less marked in the United Kingdom, certainly since the reorganisation of local government in 1974 where local government in metropolitan areas is far more highly consolidated.

Given the impact of expenditure need, tax resource imbalances and jurisdictional fragmentation, inter-governmental aid is the all-important variable which can ameliorate the deleterious effect of cumulative cycles of reinforcing impacts in public finances. It is the actions of higher-level governments, embracing both growing and declining areas, which can offset the disproportionate burdens of decline by sharing the fruits of economic growth more widely. It is higher-level government action, therefore, that prevents the rich and mobile population and healthier economic activity escaping (via spatial relocation) the burdens of supporting the poor. The critical question is, then, how far does inter-governmental aid achieve a fiscal balance between areas and hence remove the tendency for self-reinforcing impacts on public finance of city growth and decline. The answer to this question will be specific to each country depending upon the structure of public finance in that country. In the rest of this chapter a brief discussion is given of the situation in Britain.

The Geography of Local Government Finance in Britain

British local authorities, although possessing many unique characteristics, nevertheless provide an important example of the way in which jurisdictional partitioning, imposed over the pattern of aggregate social and economic change, can affect the distribution of public service costs and benefits. Indeed, it is controversy over the incidence of local revenue burdens and expenditure benefits which led in 1981 to radical reforms of local finance in Britain by the Thatcher Conservative government.

Differences in tax base

The tax base of local authorities in Britain at present consists of the rates (a form of property tax), and charges for the use of services (for example, council house rents, bus fares, etc.). Of these the rates are the most significant, although their yield has been eclipsed in recent times by the massive involvement of central government in supporting local authorities through the Rate Support Grant, as shown in Figure 5.3.

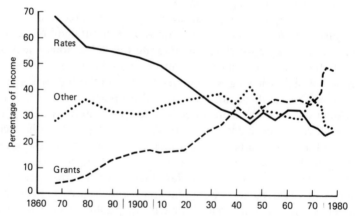

Figure 5.3   Proportion of local revenue provided by different tax sources (local current account spending only)

The rateable value of an authority measures its tax base available for revenue-raising. Hence, it is an important geographical measure of ability to pay. The variation in tax base between areas displayed in Figure 5.4 shows that high tax bases are concentrated in London and the South East, and in the central cities. These differences in the tax base arise from the variable concentration of residential and commercial property, with the commercial tax base accounting for the major part of the variation in rateable values in Britain. For example, whereas the range of total rateable value per head in

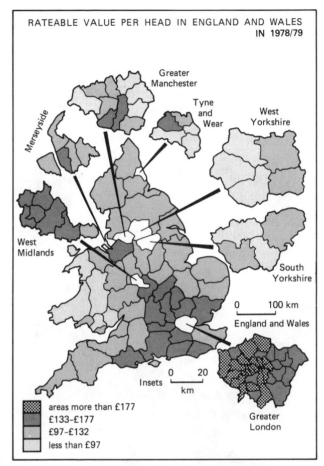

RATEABLE VALUE PER HEAD IN ENGLAND AND WALES
IN 1978/79

Greater
Manchester

Tyne
and
Wear

West
Yorkshire

Merseyside

West
Midlands

South
Yorkshire

0   100 km

England and Wales

0   20
Insets
km

areas more than £177
£133–£177
£97–£132
less than £97

Greater
London

Figure 5.4   Variation in total rateable value per head in England and
Wales in 1978–9

The figure of £177 per head was the standard below which local authorities
received distributions of Rate Support Grant in that year (resources element)

1978–9 varied from £41,000 in the City of London to £68 in
mid-Glamorgan, the range of variation in residential rateable value
per head was much less, from £232 in Westminster to £33 in
Mid-Glamorgan.

Differences in expenditure need

The expenditure need of an authority defines its requirement for revenue arising from geographical variation in concentrations of different people and industries in different areas. For example, areas that contain large numbers of schoolchildren or old people (per head of local population) place a larger burden on local

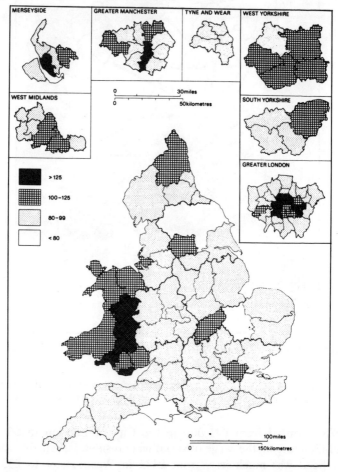

Figure 5.5   Variation in need measured per head of local population in
1978

Source: Bennett, 1982.

finances than areas with smaller numbers of these groups. As a result, such areas have higher expenditure need; and it is variation in level of *need* that becomes the geographical measure of demand for public goods.

Figure 5.5 shows one measure of variation in expenditure need. This has been defined by adding together the number of 'clients' in thirty different groups of public service categories and then weighting these clients by the costs of providing services in different locations. The result is a complex index of local authority need to spend (full details are given in Bennett, 1982). This index, although controversial in detail, show aggregate patterns which are indisputable. The result is to show the areas of highest need (per capita) to be in Inner London, most of the other older central cities, and Wales. This reflects not only the high concentration of clients in particular need groups (especially the poor, old people), but also the high cost of service provision in cities.

A further important feature is the rate of change of need to spend. This is shown in Figure 5.6 for change in aggregate need level between 1974 and 1979. The measure of need employed takes account only of current account spending requirements and hence the costs of new and renewed infrastructure (such as roads and sewers) has been excluded from this analysis. Although the rates of change are fairly small, the geographical pattern of change is very clear. The main increases in aggregate need to spend are in the rural centres and the outer metropolitan areas. This mainly reflects the pattern of population decentralisation and the growth in education needs of these areas, given their particular demographic structure; i.e. it is a manifestation of the counter-urbanisation process. The areas experiencing decline in aggregate needs are in all the central cities and the majority of inner London boroughs. These areas are experiencing very slow relative declines in need as population declines. In contrast, the more rural and suburban areas have markedly lower levels of need, but these have been slowly increasing.

Of course local authorities need not make expenditures at the level of need assessed by the index discussed above. They may choose to spend more on providing higher service quality (for example, better teacher/pupil ratios), by expanding local employment, by being less efficient, or by providing services that other authorities do not provide. Hence, when we compare actual local

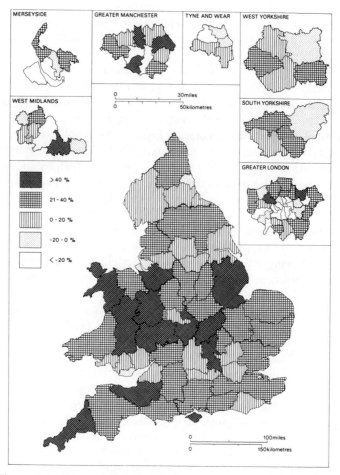

Figure 5.6   Change in level of assessed need to spend per head of population

(Change is measured over the period 1974–9 and is expressed as percentage multiplied by 100.) Source: Bennett, 1982.

spending per head in Figure 5.7 with assessed need to spend, we find a number of important differences. Many authorities, especially those in Inner London, South Yorkshire, Manchester, Newcastle and South Wales, greatly exceed their assessed spending need. This has led the Conservative central government to state that many of these authorities are 'over-spending' and as a result they have sought to penalise them through the allocation of the Rate Support Grant.

Differences in tax rates

The local tax rate is measured by the local rate poundage raised in each local authority. In aggregate this represents the ratio of the size of the local expenditures (need) to the size of the local tax base (ability to pay), after taking central grants and other transfers into

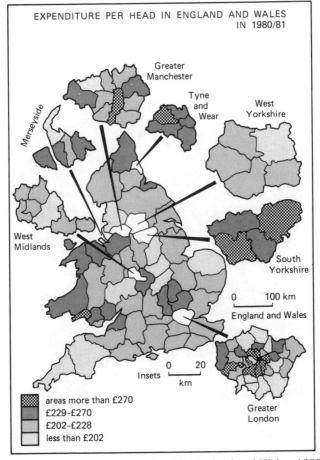

Figure 5.7   Local spending per head in England and Wales, 1980–1

account. As such it is an important measure of the variable geographical incidence of local taxation: a high rate poundage indicating a higher local tax burden than other areas on a similar class of property. As a result of these differences in rate poundages, similar income groups living in similar property can make very different contributions to local taxation depending purely on where they live. Therefore, the incidence of who gets what and pays what from public finance is a function of the geographical location: *where* they live.

Figure 5.8 shows the variation in rate poundages in different local

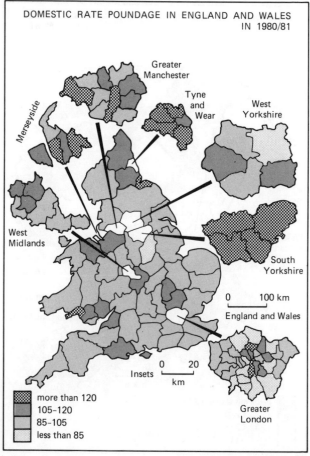

Figure 5.8   Variations in rate poundage in England and Wales, 1980–1

authorities. The variation between areas is very marked and the contrast between the metropolitan districts and most of the counties is particularly prominent. The desire and ability to raise high local poundages also depend upon local party control. Although the pattern is not entirely clear in Figure 5.8 the 'high spending' areas singled out by the Conservative government do stand out: Lambeth, Camden, Harringey, South Yorkshire, Manchester, Wigan, St Helens, Liverpool and West Glamorgan.

The equalisation problem and the history of its solution

The differential geographical distribution in Britain of tax base, expenditure need and rate poundage shows that considerable inequities in local public finance can arise purely as a result of where people live. Differences in tax bases engender differences in ability to pay and hence in the ability of local authorities to raise taxation, and this affects the local rate poundage. Differences in expenditure needs give rise to differences in the revenue that must be raised in different areas to meet the expenditure requirements, and hence again results in different rate poundages.

Governments in most Western countries have viewed as undesirable differences in the incidence of public finance burdens and benefits arising purely from the geographical choice of where people live. As a result, various equalisation programmes have been implemented by which central (or federal) governments subsidise local authorities with low tax base or high expenditure need, or both. In Britain the main mechanism by which such equalisation has been sought has been by use of central grants. Initiated in 1888, they first attained prominence under the Chamberlain government in 1929 and, as shown in Figure 5.3, have steadily grown in volume to the extent that they now account for about one half of total local spending (on both the current and capital accounts).

By far the largest equalisation grant employed in Britain is the Rate Support Grant. Initiated in 1966–7, and significantly modified for 1981–2, this alone accounts for 85 per cent of total grants and thus is responsible for 42 per cent of local current expenditure. Totalling over £12,000m in 1982–3, this is a massive item of public expenditure, equal in size to the British defence budget, and is the largest single programme in Britain that has an explicit *geographical* focus (see Bennett, 1982).

Table 5.1 Variations in grant from central government

	Fiscal year	Total grants per head vs. RV/head (excluding City and Westminster)	Total grant vs. resources expenditures	Total grant per head vs. average local wages[†] (×100)
General grant and rate deficiency grant	1962–3	−1.563*	0.380*	−0.132
	1965–6	−0.265*	0.160*	−0.089*
Rate support grant	1967–8	−0.554*	0.233*	−0.055
	1969–70	−0.315*	0.359*	−0.046
	1971–2	−0.492*	0.004	−0.057
	1973–4	−0.213*	0.442*	−0.036
	1974–5	−0.106*	0.498*	−0.479*
	1975–6	−0.200*	0.209*	−1.049*
	1976–7	−0.106*	0.373*	−0.332*
	1977–8	−0.122*	0.360*	−0.126*
	1978–9	−0.037*	0.401*	0.621
	1979–80	−0.071	0.354*	0.500
	1980–1	−0.136*	0.346*	0.371

* Significant at the 90% level.
† Pre-1974 wage regressions are on a reduced data set using 1974 wage data.

Table 5.1 displays the aggregate relation of the Rate Support Grant to tax base, expenditure level, and local wage levels for selected years. In addition this table also shows the same relation for the previous grant system of the General Grant and Rate Deficiency Grant which was replaced by the Rate Support Grant in 1966–7. This table shows that since 1974–5 the grant became steadily less redistributive with respect to both local tax base and local personal incomes. This mainly reflects the aims of the Labour government of this period to channel aid preferentially to the cities which (in general) possess the higher tax bases and higher income earners. However, since 1973–4, the grant has been relatively stable in distribution with respect to expenditure levels. For the most recent years, since 1980–1, the grant has become markedly less redistributive towards the areas with low tax base and the areas with high expenditure levels, reflecting the Conservative government's aim of reducing grant levels in many high-spending areas, especially in cities.

There have been considerable criticisms of the manner of distribution of the Rate Support Grant ever since its inception, and these have not been abated by its reform in 1981–2. Despite these criticisms, it can be concluded from the results of Table 5.1 that the Rate Support Grant has been very significant in achieving a level of equalisation of tax burdens and expenditure benefits. However, it is clear from the evolution and changes in aggregate grant distribution shown in this table that the grant has been to some extent a political football which has suffered changes in priorities as to the level of tax base or expenditure equalisation that has been accorded. It remains to be seen how far the reforms of 1981–2 that have generated so much controversy will be maintained in future grant allocations. Whatever the results of future changes, it is certain that shifts in Rate Support Grant will affect local tax rates and local expenditures; and hence will affect who gets what where, and at what cost from the public services.

6
Public Provision and the Quality of Life

Paul L. Knox and Andrew Kirby

The problems of operating an equitable yet efficient welfare state have long given cause for concern. One problem which is not always recognised, however, is the variability of public provision between different parts of the country. This is true at all spatial scales. Some regions have more hospital facilities and doctors per person than others; some cities spend much more on education than others; and some neighbourhoods enjoy better amenities than others. All in all, what may simply be an accident of birth in a particular area can ultimately have an enormous effect upon an individual's well-being. Of course, the uneven distribution of indigent and vulnerable persons and households means that the *need* for public provision also varies from place to place. The critical question, therefore, is whether variations in provision match variations in the type and intensity of need. Figure 6.1, for example, shows the broad variations that exist in what have been called 'levels of living', using an index based on three variables: unemployment, perinatal mortality, and average earnings. The overall pattern reflected by this yardstick is a polarisation either side of the Severn–Humber divide, with the best conditions occurring in the South East and the worst in Northern Ireland and the metropolitan regions of South Wales, Scotland and Northern and Midland England. A recent analysis of Britain's cities has emphasised the distinctions which exist in the *nature* of the socio-economic environment as well as in the overall level of living (Donnison and Soto, 1980). Thirteen different groups of cities were identified on the basis of a broad spectrum of socio-economic variables: regional service centres, resorts, residential suburbs, new industrial suburbs, new towns, Welsh mining towns, heavy-engineering/coal towns, inner conurbations, two kinds of engineering towns, the towns of central Scotland, and London. At a more general level, these fall into one of two broad categories: 'traditional Britain' and 'new Britain'. The significant feature about the division is that the towns and cities of 'new Britain' – the new towns, new industrial suburbs, resorts, regional service centres and London – are generally more prosperous and *egalitarian*: for any given occupational group, opportunity

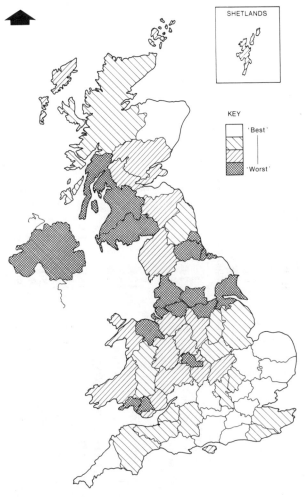

Figure 6.1   Variations in levels of living

Table 6.1 Unemployment and car ownership by city type and occupational group, 1971

	Unemployment (UK = 100)					Cars per household (UK = 100)				
	Professional and managerial	Other non-manual	Skilled manual	Semi-skilled manual	Unskilled manual	Professional and managerial	Other non-manual	Skilled manual	Semi-skilled manual	Unskilled manual
'NEW BRITAIN'										
New industrial suburbs	93	79	63	61	64	115	131	126	137	152
Residential suburbs	64	67	53	64	60	129	153	156	160	181
London	92	94	81	69	55	98	93	115	105	128
New towns	75	62	52	52	48	119	146	146	169	187
Regional service centres	108	104	96	106	90	95	99	102	101	112
Resorts	158	165	109	118	108	91	95	113	101	119
'TRADITIONAL BRITAIN'										
Central Scotland	157	161	210	209	228	79	65	55	50	43
Welsh mining towns	145	145	163	152	169	76	85	74	97	96
Inner conurbations	118	121	132	130	133	88	82	80	77	67
Heavy engineering/coal	87	80	95	96	96	101	111	91	103	97
Textile towns	94	94	92	102	96	96	95	86	76	71
Engineering I	105	90	92	85	89	97	101	91	98	99
Engineering II	95	88	88	94	97	105	118	115	132	123

Source: Extracted from Donnison and Soto, 1980, pp. 109–11.

and affluence tend to be greater than in the towns and cities of 'traditional Britain' (Table 6.1).

Clearly, then, the agencies responsible for the welfare state are faced with different demands from place to place. In those sectors for which local authorities are responsible (these include the provision of housing, education, social services and transport), the pattern of expenditure seems broadly to reflect these needs, although these data are not necessarily an entirely accurate measure of either the level or quality of service provision. This, in turn, reflects the 'needs' element employed in calculating the allocation of the Rate Support Grant to local authorities by the central government. Figure 6.2 shows the distribution of local authorities in England and Wales in terms of 'spenders' and 'stinters'. As we can see, many of the spenders are found in areas having a relatively low level of living. There is a critical difference, however, between the high spenders with rich potential for generating their own revenue – Buckinghamshire, Shropshire, Manchester, Brent – and the 'poor spenders', which have to deal with low incomes, high unemployment and poor housing without being able to draw on a very substantial local tax base – for example, Dyfed, Huddersfield, Northumberland, Oldham, Rochdale, Sheffield and West Glamorgan.

Local authorities also vary in the *pattern* of their expenditure on different services and amenities. Welsh local authorities, for example, have traditionally spent a high proportion of their total budget on education, while the spending pattern of Scottish local authorities has been dominated by the provision and maintenance of public housing. Such differences in expenditure patterns are attributable to a variety of factors, including the political complexion of the local council, the functional centrality of the authority (i.e., its role as a central place), as well as the nature and intensity of local needs for different services. Research on local authority performance in the United Kingdom suggests that there are two distinctive types of area (Newton, 1976). In the first, a declining industrial base is associated with poor housing and adverse environmental conditions, a youthful, working-class population, and Labour party control. Within their total budget they tend to spend lower-than-average amounts on parks, police and roads but higher-than-average amounts on health, housing, mothers and young children, primary education and special education. In

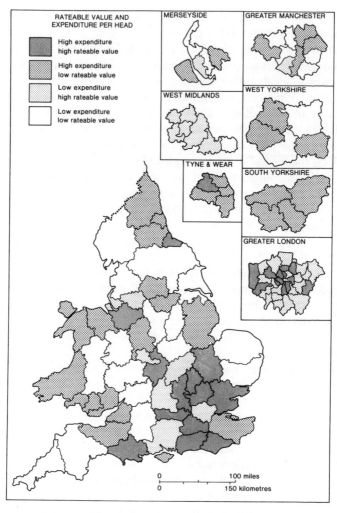

Figure 6.2　Spenders and stinters

Source:　Bennett (1982).

general, therefore, they spend more on socially ameliorative and
redistributive services but less on 'caretaker' services. The second
type of area is characteristically an affluent residential or commercial community with an ageing, middle-class population and a
Conservative-controlled council. Here, the pattern of spending is

reversed, with relatively more being spent on public goods such as roads, while 'divisible' services such as housing, health services, personal social services and education receive less.

These patterns are not static however, and the changes that have been taking place over the last decade are reinforcing the emergence of very different types of local authority. Tighter controls on allocation within the Rate Support Grant have particularly hit at the Metropolitan Counties and the London Boroughs. The withdrawal of funds from regional aid has further damaged those authorities with a weak industrial structure; a change in the boundaries of the Assisted Areas means that many authorities are, moreover, no longer even eligible to compete for cash. Third, as Taylor and Johnston indicate elsewhere in this volume, personal tax changes have systematically released growing amounts of disposable income into the local economies of the already affluent regions, at the expense of the traditionally weaker ones. Together, these tendencies mean that the local authorities with the weakest financial bases are suffering further erosion, while the healthiest are enjoying even better prospects.

In short, both the size and the composition of the 'social wage' derived from local authority provision depend very much on where one lives. In this context, one of the most interesting suggestions to emerge from analysis of spatial variations in needs and public provision is that there exists a type of place – the 'good city' – in which the most vulnerable members of society tend to suffer less than they do elsewhere, even though they may represent a larger proportion of the local population (Donnison and Soto, 1980). Such places, it is suggested, also provide a better educational environment than most others, together with a generally high standard of public services. What is most surprising about them is that they are not part of the affluent 'new Britain'. Rather, they are part of 'middle England': places such as Rochester and Chatham, Thurrock, Peterborough, and Swindon. Such places, although 'good cities' in terms of providing a 'kinder' and more equal environment, do not exhibit the imprint of elegant living or conspicuous consumption: they have few good cultural facilities, few buildings listed as worthy of preservation, few specialist shops catering for the tastes of the upper-middle classes, and no entry in the *Good Food Guide*.

Local authorities represent only one channel of public provision, however. Patterns of central government expenditure also exhibit a high degree of spatial variability which does not always match patterns of need. A good example is the provision of medical care. Despite the fact that one of the founding principles of the National Health Service was geographical equality of provision, and despite the complex formulae employed by its Resource Allocation Working Party in an attempt to account for local needs, sharp disparities in provision have persisted and, in some cases, intensified (Black Report, 1982; Knox, 1979). Moreover, these disparities have been shown to amount to a serious mismatch between needs and resources – a mismatch that is compounding many of the longstanding and well-documented social and geographical gradients in mortality, morbidity and the quality of life in general. Julian Hart, a practising general practitioner, succinctly summed up this trend in terms of an 'inverse care law', whereby 'the availability of good medical care tends to vary inversely with the need of the population

Table 6.2   Variations in need and provision, regional health authorities, 1978

RHA	Available beds/1000 population (England $\bar{X}$:8.1)	Distribution of RHA expenditure (England = 100%)	Predicted distribution (*see below)
Northern	8.4	6.36	7.06
Yorkshire	8.6	7.19	7.78
Trent	7.1	8.80	9.53
E Anglia	7.2	3.57	3.81
NW Thames	8.5	8.54	6.96
NE Thames	8.4	8.71	8.18
SE Thames	8.4	8.58	7.92
SW Thames	9.5	6.80	6.16
Wessex	7.3	5.26	5.44
Oxford	6.3	4.30	4.10
S Western	8.4	6.34	6.96
W Midlands	7.2	9.73	10.73
Mersey	9.3	5.56	5.56
N Western	7.8	9.19	9.82

* These data are taken from Palmer *et al.*, 1980, and are estimates for 1978–9 based on SMRs: these Standardised Morality Ratios take into account the variations in death rate between regions, corrected for age and sex distributions. they thus represent a crude measure of health and ill-health within regions.
Source: Compiled from CSO Statistics, 1980.

served' (Hart, 1971). Such a 'law' is something of an overstatement, though there is a good deal of evidence that not only points to the existence of steep regional gradients in the provision of medical care, but also demonstrates a weak, if not exactly inverse, relationship with patterns of need. In Table 6.2, for example, we can see the variations that exist between Regional Health Authorities *vis-à-vis* hospital provision. In column one, the standardised availability of hospital beds is seen to be higher than the national average in the four London RHAs, and in the Northern, Yorkshire and South Western Authorities (occupation figures show a similar distribution). This kind of measure can then be related to some notion of medical need. In columns two and three, for example, are the proportions of the total budget allocated to each RHA in 1978, and the proportions that are predicted using data on the demand for medical care.

Figure 6.3a Regional health authorities' variations in need and provision

It can be seen that the reallocation exercise begun in 1976 under the RAWP proposals has ironed out some of the major variations between regions, but that inequities still remain; in particular the London RHAs appear overfinanced in relation to, for example, the West Midlands (such a statement does not imply of course that even the most affluent RHAs necessarily have funds which are fully adequate: Eyles *et al*., 1982). These data are summarised in Figures 6.3a and 6.3b.

Similarly, regional variations still exist in the provision of primary care (Table 6.3). Indeed, a recent report by the Department of Health and Social Security (1978) suggests that 2,000 more physicians will be needed over the next twenty years simply to redress regional disparities in medical manpower. As in the other spheres we have examined, policy frameworks aimed at preventing

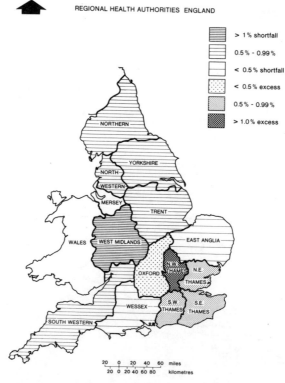

Figure 6.3b   Regional health authorities' variations in need and provision

Table 6.3   Regional variations in levels of primary care in 1981

	Average list size	% of Principals with a caseload of 2,000 or more
ENGLAND (Regional Health Authorities):		
Northern	2237	30
Yorkshire	2186	26
Trent	2309	38
East Anglia	2118	15
NW Thames	2194	31
NE Thames	2221	29
SE Thames	2197	31
SW Thames	2215	27
Oxford	2102	16
South West	2221	27
West Midlands	2053	14
Mersey	2233	31
North West	2210	30
Wessex	2102	33
SCOTLAND (Health Board Areas):		
Argyll and Clyde	1721	1
Ayr and Arran	1899	1
Borders	1593	0
Dumfries and Galloway	1652	1
Fife	1951	1
Forth Valley	1836	1
Grampian	1863	1
Greater Glasgow	1872	3
Highland	1422	1
Lanarkshire	2182	3
Lothian	1801	1
Orkney	968	1
Shetland	1336	0
Tayside	1846	1
Western Isles	1364	0

Source: Department of Health and Social Services, *Health and Personal Social Services Statistics*; Scottish Health Department, *Scottish Health Statistics*.

geographical imbalances do exist. General practitioners are not permitted to practise in areas where the average caseload of existing family doctors is less than 1,800, and are actively encouraged, through cash incentives, to practise in areas where the average caseload is more than 2,500. The districts used in implementing this policy have been insufficiently sensitive to local variations in the need for primary care, however. Moreover, most young doctors are indifferent to the financial incentives to work in depressed regions, unmoved by the idea of working with needy or vulnerable populations, and ignorant of the location of 'under-' and 'over-doctored' areas (Butler and Knight, 1974; Knox and Pacione, 1980). Within the medical profession, general practice in working-class districts is not only held to be unglamorous and unsatisfying but also to be an impediment to career advancement. Medical manpower therefore continues to be attracted to locations that offer pleasant and prosperous surroundings, where there are opportunities to indulge in private practice, and where there is a reasonable degree of proximity to specialised hospital facilities.

Similarly, the more deprived neighbourhoods of towns and cities tend to be persistently under-doctored. At this scale the locational behaviour of family doctors is also influenced by 'fabric' effects which tend to reinforce the relative advantages enjoyed by established middle-class neighbourhoods. There is, for instance, an almost complete lack of accommodation suitable for use as doctors' surgeries in the large housing estates – both public and private – which have encircled most British cities since 1945. Purpose-built Health Centres have been established in some of the suburban neighbourhoods of some cities in recent years. But the rationalisation of practices involved in setting up Health Centres inevitably means that economies of scale are achieved at the expense of equity in patients' accessibility to primary care. Figure 6.4, which shows the distribution of general practitioners in Edinburgh, illustrates the typical outcome: high levels of provision in inner-city neighbourhoods of all kinds, low levels of provision in peripheral public housing schemes and newer owner-occupied neighbourhoods, and intermediate levels of provision in higher-status large-established owner-occupied neighbourhoods.

This last example highlights two of the problems that consistently emerge in studies of resource allocation. The first is making sure that provision keeps pace with population change. As John Goddard showed in Chapter 4, British cities have experienced enormous shifts of people in recent years. Figure 6.4 reflects the way that services often persist in areas of past population concentration – inner-city neighbourhoods – but are slow to be provided in newly populated areas – new suburban developments. Even in

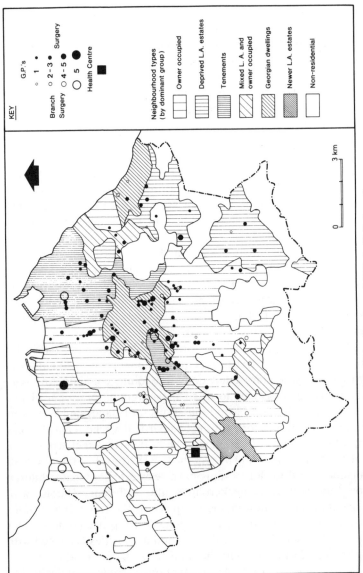

Figure 6.4   Distribution of GPs in Edinburgh

smaller cities and towns this means that some households (particularly the aged, the infirm, single parents, and those without private transport) have difficulty in getting to doctors, dentists, libraries and other amenities, with the result that they may use such services less than they might. Where health is concerned, this may of course turn minor problems into major ones (Knox, 1979).

The second problem is that of making sure that all services are of an equally high standard. Here again there is a tendency towards regressive spatial patterns. Surveys of medical care in cities, for example, have shown that general practitioners in working-class neighbourhoods tend to have heavier caseloads than those in middle-class neighbourhoods, that only half as many have further qualifications, that less than one-fifth as many have access to physiotherapy facilities, only half as many hold hospital appointments or have access to hospital beds in which they could care for their own patients, and only one-third as many manage to visit their patients when they are in hospital under specialist care. Moreover, many inner-city neighbourhoods with relatively high levels of medical manpower turn out to be served by disproportionate numbers of elderly physicians operating single-handedly from poorly equipped lock-up surgeries whose ambience is itself a deterrent to many patients (Knox, 1982a).

The issue of the *quality* of provision has assumed particular importance with respect to a major component of local authority provision – secondary education. It is quite common for some schools within a local authority to attract reputations for academic excellence while others gain reputations for truancy and low levels of achievement. In short, getting to a particular school may be very important in terms of attainment, and often the 'right school' is a matter of where the child lives in the city (Kirby, 1982). In the past, catchment and feeder systems have served to segregate children from different class backgrounds into different schools, with residential segregation taking the place of the less subtle 11-plus examination as a means of separation. This approach is now under some public scrutiny as local education authorities are faced with the choice of which schools should be closed, due to falling rolls.

In Reading, for example, a situation of some complexity has arisen, as a result of previous educational gerrymandering (Figure 6.5). Catchment A, it can be seen, is an artificial geographical unit which crosses the CBD and ensures that very long distances are

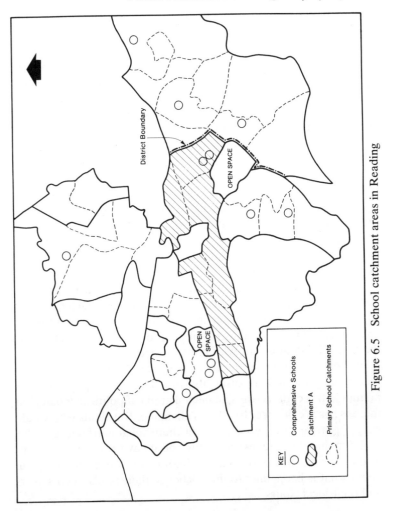

Figure 6.5   School catchment areas in Reading

travelled by some pupils. Its only apparent rationale is that it contains a high proportion of the town's black and Asian neighbourhoods, with the result that nearly half of the 1980 intake into the two comprehensives in catchment A came from these ethnic minorities (cf. a city-wide proportion of approximately 7 per cent). These two schools (one boys', one girls') are now faced with closure due to their poor educational performance, which belatedly poses real threats to the racial integrity of neighbouring schools, that will for the first time have to integrate their intake. One irony within this development is that although falling rolls exist within Reading, neighbouring suburban schools in Wokingham District, to the east of Reading, are suffering unprecedented expansion. Despite the fact that the district boundary does not cross a county boundary (i.e. both districts are within the same LEA) there has never been any attempt to confront the political resistance that exists within many suburban communities to the sanctity of their schools.

This example, in turn, highlights the role of local authority bureaucrats as 'gatekeepers' in relation to publicly provided services and amenities. The allocation of public housing provides a particularly good example here. Not only are the available housing opportunities rationed out through a variety of eligibility rules and priority systems, but different *kinds* of accommodation, in different kinds of neighbourhoods, are offered to different kinds of households on the basis of evaluations by 'street-level bureaucrats': housing visitors and the like. In this way, public officials are effectively able to determine much of what contributes to a household's quality of life, since a particular residential location, as we have seen, is not only set in a particular physical and social environment but is also the critical point of reference in relation to the accessibility of a variety of public services.

In short, variations in the social wage can be very important in determining the quality of an individual's life. At present, local politics in this country are a neglected arena of political debate, but there is some evidence that this is changing. Residents who would never approve of a peace camp in their neighbourhood are also realising that they are also unhappy about having nuclear weapons in their area, while apolitical neighbours are moved to complain about what is happening to their schools, their roads, their sewers and their local clinics.

7
Energy Issues

Peter R. Odell

For almost two hundred years after the mid-eighteenth century, the economic development of Britain was closely related to the exploitation of its large and extensive coal resources. Increasing levels of production were achieved from deeper and deeper reserves and the coal produced was applied to a widening range of uses. In addition to its direct use in manufacturing industry, indigenous coal heated most of the nation's homes, supplied motive power for the railways, and at a later stage was used almost exclusively for electricity production, and also provided the raw material for the chemical industry. Until after the Second World War, Britain's coalmining areas still constituted most of the country's principal centres of population and industry.

The Decline of Coal

In the aftermath of the Second World War, when the coal industry was in a run-down state and at a time when demand was growing rapidly, Britain was short of energy. The solution to the problem was then more or less generally thought to lie in the rapid rehabilitation of the war-scarred coal industry, the massive expansion of which was thus planned and projected. This was the responsibility of the country's newly nationalised coal industry, which through a large investment programme and the incentive of high wages to the labour force sought to expand output by almost a third to some 240 million tons per year. Meanwhile, however, there were insufficient supplies to meet customers' needs. Coal imports thus had to be encouraged, and this measure, together with the fiscal and other incentives designed to enhance the flow of crude oil and oil products to meet some of Britain's energy needs, were viewed essentially as short-term expedients by energy policy-makers. The imports would, it was predicated, simply help out temporarily and give the time necessary to enable the British coal industry to be put back into shape through a massive programme of investment in the mines, and by the rejuvenation of the ageing mining force of the immediate post-war period.

Contrary to these expectations, however, from about 1955, with but a brief respite at the time of the first Arab/Israeli conflict in 1957, the British coal industry was fighting to retain its markets in the face of increasingly severe competition from oil. Paradoxically, this fight was not even in the context of a declining demand for energy, but rather in a period when energy use increased rapidly as a result of a growing economy, which under the impact of expanded industrialisation, electrification, motorisation and rising living standards, was becoming more and more energy-intensive.

Competition from Imported Oil

It was, indeed, in part the too-rapid rate of growth in energy use at that time that caused the crisis for coal. The coal industry was simply unable to respond adequately to the increasing energy demands of users whose confidence in coal was therefore undermined. This made most consumers more than willing to respond positively to the growing efforts of an increasing number of international oil companies to supply them with the energy they needed. The economies of scale the oil companies thus achieved in transporting oil to Britain, and in refining and distributing it within the country, enabled the oil industry to break through cost-barrier after cost-barrier. Even more important, the industry had access to the then seemingly limitless supplies of low- and decreasing-price crude oil from the prolific fields of the Middle East and North Africa, etc. As shown in Figure 7.1, the 'real' price of Saudi-Arabian light crude oil fell by over 60 per cent between 1950 and 1970. Oil products thus became available to industrial, commercial and residential users at prices with which most of British coal production could not compete, given especially the rising real cost of labour in an industry in which wages accounted for over 50 per cent of total costs. In addition there were the costs of closing surplus production capacity,

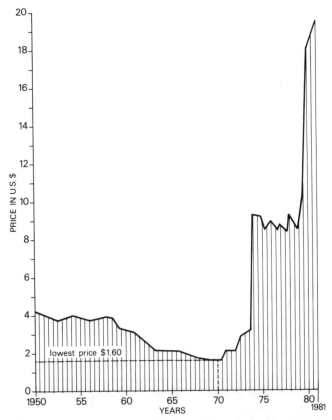

Figure 7.1   The price of Saudi-Arabian light crude oil, 1950–80 (in
constant 1974 dollars)

most of which had to be met directly by the NCB. By the end of the
1960s the UK coal industry was less than two-thirds of the size it had
been a decade earlier – and it was still contracting. In 1971, after
fifteen years of competition, oil became a more important source of
energy in the United Kingdom's economy than coal – in spite of
progressive government subsidies and the creation of protected
markets for the British coal industry, notably in electricity production. This change in the fortunes of the two industries is shown in
Figure 7.2.

The decline in coal production was not, of course, the result of the
depletion of Britain's coal resources – nor even of a decline in the

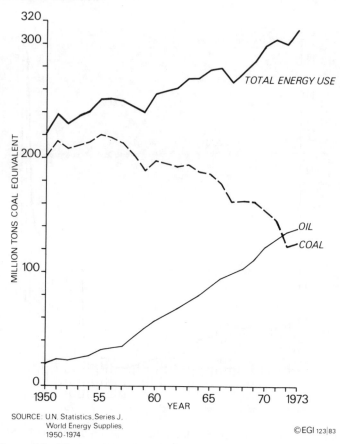

SOURCE: U.N. Statistics, Series J,
World Energy Supplies,
1950-1974

©EGI 123|83

Figure 7.2   The use of coal and oil in the United Kingdom, 1950–73

accessibility of known reserves of coal (except in a few special cases, such as Durham coking coal and South Wales anthracite). Throughout most of the coalfields, potentially productive pits were closed in order to bring production capacity more into balance with declining demand.

The clear inability for Britain's coal resources to be produced at a level of costs that enabled them to compete for markets with oil products (except for power generation in the vicinity of the continent's lowest-cost coalfields, such as those of the East Midlands and South Yorkshire), and the apparent absence of any other plentiful indigenous sources of energy, led to an evaluation that

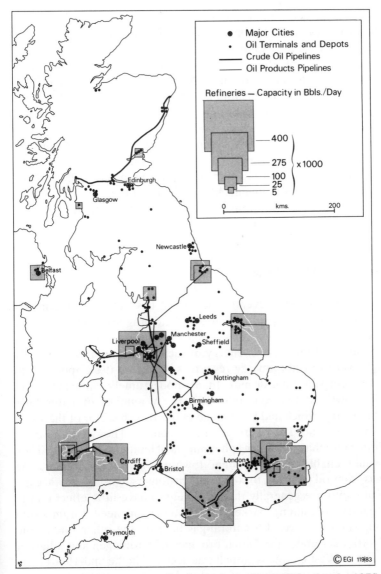

Figure 7.3   The downstream oil industry in the United Kingdom by 1973

Britain was an energy-poor country. The economy's growing energy needs were destined, it was generally argued, to become increasingly dependent upon the willingness of the world's oil-rich countries (and the twenty or so international oil companies responsible for the exploitation of those countries' oil resources) to continue to supply Britain with rising volumes of crude oil. By 1972, annual imports of oil exceeded 100 million tons (imports had been less than 7 per cent of this volume only twenty years earlier), and the generally accepted view was that oil imports would continue to rise. Over 150 million tons were anticipated by 1980, and 300 million tons or more by the end of the century! The import terminals, refineries, inland pipelines and associated transport facilities which had grown from small and unimportant phenomena in 1950 to large and extensive developments in many parts of the country by 1972, as shown in Figure 7.3, thus seemed destined to continue to expand for the rest of the century.

Indigenous Oil and Gas

A set of traumatic events since 1972 has entirely undermined those earlier energy sector diagnoses and prognoses. The pre-1973 expectations that high growth rates in energy use would persist, involved a future use of energy of such large dimensions that any discoveries of new energy resources in Britain itself appeared to offer prospects for little more than a modest amelioration in the rate of growth in the country's imports. A number of natural-gas discoveries which had been made in the British sector of the south North Sea since 1964 were seen in this context. They were viewed as little more than interesting phenomena of limited significance. They would enable the traditional town-gas and its successor, the gas-from-oil industry, to convert its customers to using natural gas – but they were generally thought likely to have little effect on the country's remaining markets for coal and rising needs for imported oil. The existence of a natural-gas field on the other side of the North Sea, under the Dutch province of Groningen and adjacent parts of West Germany, which was declared in the mid-1960s to be one of the non-communist-world's largest accumulations of gas (containing over 2,500 million tons of coal equivalent), was not widely recognised as being of significance in the evaluation of the

United Kingdom's gas resources. Its size and its other attributes indicated a much greater than hitherto expected potential for hydrocarbon resources throughout the sedimentary areas of North West Europe. This applied particularly to the North Sea petroliferous province in which, geologically, the Groningen gas field was located (at the southern extremity), with the larger part of the province lying offshore the eastern coastline of the United Kingdom.

The North Sea Oil and Gas Province

Legal agreements between the surrounding countries over the division of these countries' rights to the mineral resources under the North Sea (as shown in Figure 7.4), and legislation for concession agreements between governments and companies, created the conditions in which the offshore exploration effort for oil and gas could begin. Technologically, however, the North Sea was a 'frontier region' for oil and gas exploitation, so that progress was, at first, necessarily slow and tentative. Nevertheless, by the time of the oil 'crisis' in 1973, sufficient work had been done and enough success achieved already to make it clear that the North Sea was likely to be a major oil and gas province by international standards. All its sectors, but especially those of Britain and Norway, quickly proved to be prolific to a very encouraging extent. The much higher price of oil, moreover, in the aftermath of the 1973 oil crisis, stimulated its exploration and exploitation. Today, less than twenty years since the discovery of the first offshore gas field, the North Sea oil and gas province is proven as one of the world's most important in terms of the number and size of the fields, as shown in Figures 7.5 and 7.6. Over 20 giant fields (with over 500 million barrels of oil and/or oil equivalent) have already been proven and a smaller number remain to be found. In total there are at least 300 oil and/or gas discoveries in the North Sea of which about 60 are already producing or being developed for production – mainly in the British sector, where developments have proceeded faster than elsewhere.

Major petroliferous provinces, by world standards, such as that under the North Sea and adjacent areas, do not reveal their ultimate 'secrets' as far as eventual reserves, potential production levels, and the longevity of production are concerned in the first twenty years

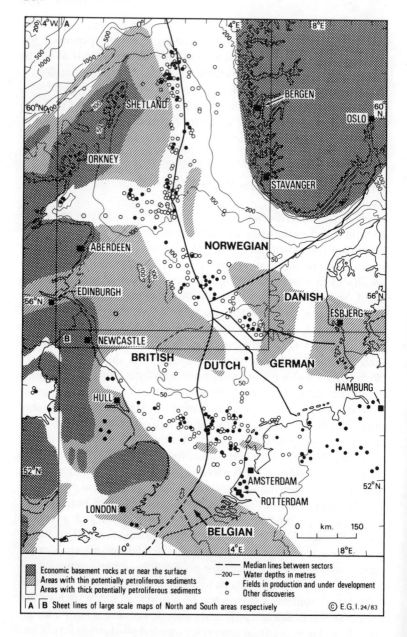

Figure 7.4   The North Sea oil and gas province

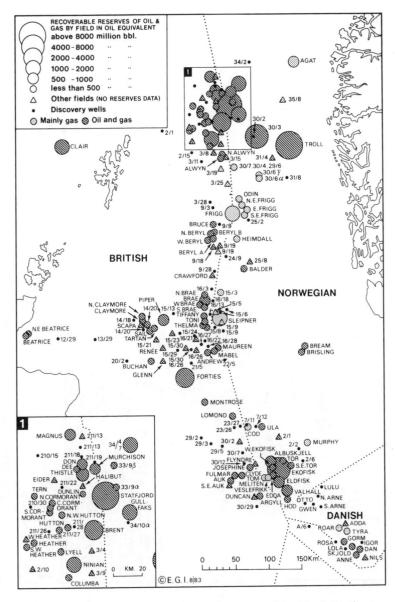

Figure 7.5   Oil and gas fields in the northern part of the North Sea (sector A on Figure 7.4)

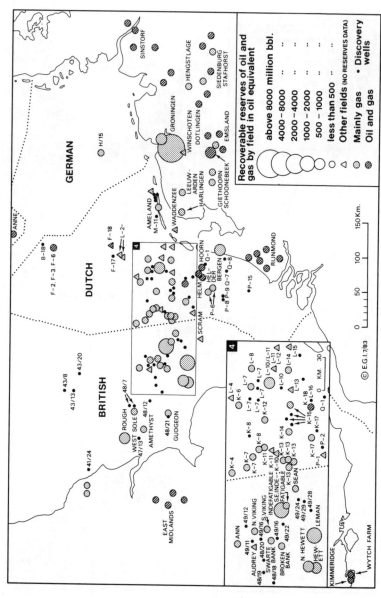

Figure 7.6   Oil and gas fields in the southern part of the North Sea (sector B on Figure 7.4)

of their exploration and exploitation. The 'life' of such an extensive and complicated petroliferous province extends over many decades. For the whole of this period it is the process of the exploitation of the oil and gas – that is, the production, or the 'depletion' as it is often termed, of the discovered and declared reserves – that ensures the continuation of reserves' expansion through new discoveries and the re-evaluation of old fields. In such a 'positive' approach to the exploration and exploitation of a major province the challenges of the nuances of its complex geology and the characteristics of the varying types of reservoirs are gradually sorted out. Thus, opportunities for reappraising the reserves and the production potential are *successively* opened up over many decades on a more or less continuing basis.

Unhappily, this phenomenon of a very extended period of evaluation – providing exploitation continues to be encouraged – is not widely appreciated in the United Kingdom, where unfamiliarity with the industry, and a firmly held belief in the idea of the country as energy-poor – coupled with inappropriate styles of government intervention and penal fiscal policies as far as the oil industry is concerned – have led to a situation in which the essential continuity of the discovery and the production process has been inhibited. This has led inevitably to an under-declaration of the reserves' potential and of their production capabilities. Thus, south North Sea gas reserves which have been discovered in large quantities remain unexploited because of successive governments' and British Gas's restrictive production and marketing policies for natural gas, and because the companies that have found the gas were, until recently, denied a price for it that justified their investing in its exploitation. Similarly, excessively high rates of taxation, which are not related to the profitability of individual fields, have inhibited the development of the smaller and/or less accessible fields, especially those in the deeper waters of the northern North Sea.

Nevertheless, within the context of the failure of energy use in general to expand since 1973 in Britain because of adverse economic conditions (Britain's use in 1982 was down to only two-thirds of its use in 1972), even the relatively slow and modest exploitation to date of British North Sea oil and gas reserves has enabled them to expand to meet over 55 per cent of Britain's total energy needs. Indeed, their joint contribution to the country's total energy supply (including exports) is now almost twice that of the British coal industry.

Oil and Gas Resources Development Policies

The United Kingdom has now become more than self-sufficient in oil and also produces most of the natural gas that it consumes. It has, moreover, the potential for continuing to expand its oil and gas production for at least the rest of the century. The oil and gas reserves already proven or probable offer this potential (though this is not widely realised because of the policies of constraint on the development of the reserves that have been imposed), and beyond this there is scope for further expansion based on the yet-to-be-discovered reserves. In the United States, long experience in oil and gas exploitation has demonstrated the validity of the concept of 'undiscovered but discoverable reserves' when taking decisions on appropriate future production levels. For British policy-makers, the concept is little known, and even less accepted as an appropriate basis for oil and gas production planning. Instead, production plans for periods of up to twenty-five years are based on the highly constrained concept of proven reserves only. As a result, the rate of production is kept below the level that could be achieved. Furthermore, as the production process is the essential means whereby continuity in finding new reserves in a maturing province can be ensured, the reserves' discovery process is also constrained. Thus the contribution of indigenous oil and gas to the energy needs of Britain is being kept, and will continue to be held, below the level that might otherwise be achieved.

Ironically, this failure properly to exploit the country's oil and gas resources is usually claimed to be an achievement! The limitation on production is presented as a willingness to curb the 'greed' of present-day potential users of the resources in favour of tomorrow's claimants. Superficially attractive though this idea may appear to be (it is presented as a 'conservationist' approach, made in a spirit of responsibility to the needs of future generations), its validity is, in reality, undermined by the fact that the failure to encourage or to allow production today necessarily creates an inability in the longer term to find the new reserves, given a continuing exploration effort. Instead, the economic motivation to find new oil and gas is diminished – or even eliminated – and thus the prospects for the expansion – or even the maintenance – of production are severely affected. The field development process is slowed down, so the North Sea oil and gas province, with its many remaining undiscovered but discoverable resources, is in danger of being prematurely abandoned. This, of course, must be at the cost of all concerned, including those future generations whose interests in the resources the conservationists claim to be seeking to protect. Paradoxical though it may seem, the interest of future generations, in respect of their access to supplies of indigenous oil and gas, are best served by maximising production in the short term. Unfortunately, Britain's policies in limiting immediate oil and gas production levels are undermining the chances of our children and grandchildren also being able to benefit from the availability of indigenous supplies.

A 'Comeback' for Indigenous Coal?

The hesitancy in developing British oil and gas resources to the fullest possible extent can also be related to the post-1973 situation for the UK coal industry. Following its severe cutback in the period from the late 1950s to the early 1970s, the coal industry came to enjoy something of a resurgence of interest – in the aftermath of the oil price rises and enhanced fears over the security of energy supplies. As a result, it was able to lay claim to special treatment – for example, in terms of guaranteed markets for its output and of access to capital for new projects – despite the following considerations. First, the real resource costs involved in exploiting new British coal reserves are much greater than those involved in the exploitation of even high-cost offshore oil and gas; and second, other OECD countries (notably Canada, the United States and Australia), plus other nations of the non-communist world (for example, South Africa, Colombia, Indonesia), have vast quantities of inherently lower-cost coal available, or potentially available, for export to coal-consuming countries. The growing competition between these alternative suppliers, plus the economies of scale yet to be achieved in coal production and transport, is, moreover, likely to keep real prices stable, or even to bring them down.

In this context the continued upward pressure of wage and

interest costs on the price of British coal output over the rest of the century seems likely to make the large-scale redevelopment of the remaining extensive indigenous coal resources a relatively 'bad buy' for the consumers involved. This is notably the case for the electricity supply industry, which has decided to base its expansion on nuclear power production, in spite of the widespread concern for the real costs involved in such a policy, and the even greater concern for the safety of the power stations and the transport and processing of nuclear waste in a country as crowded as Britain. Indeed, most of Britain's large remaining resources of deep coal should, realistically, be viewed only as a potential resource, with the best prospects for its ultimate use depending on the development of a successful method for its underground gasification. This is an early-twenty-first-century prospect at best. In the meantime, the protection extended to the traditional coal industry not only serves to inhibit oil and gas resources' exploitation, but it also constrains the efforts required to achieve the technological breakthrough to underground gasification.

Constraints on Resource Development

To return, however, to the oil and gas resources themselves; and to a number of institutional and fiscal considerations adversely affecting development in Britain. Institutionally, the high degree of centralised ownership and/or control over the resources is an inhibiting factor. Indeed, the national ownership of mineral rights very effectively reduces the opportunity and the motivation for the exploitation of all but the largest accumulations of on-shore oil and gas. This is in a situation in which most of the country's on-shore oil and gas resources remain to be discovered, as a result of new geological knowledge and of improved methods of exploration. These resources are likely to be found mainly in medium or small fields scattered over large parts of southern and eastern England – as shown in Figure 7.7. As neither individual landowners, nor the local communities concerned, secure much, if anything, by way of direct financial return from the production of oil and gas under 'their' land, the inconvenience and/or pollution that is necessarily involved in such activities usually stimulates local opposition to any development proposals that may be made (see Chapter 10).

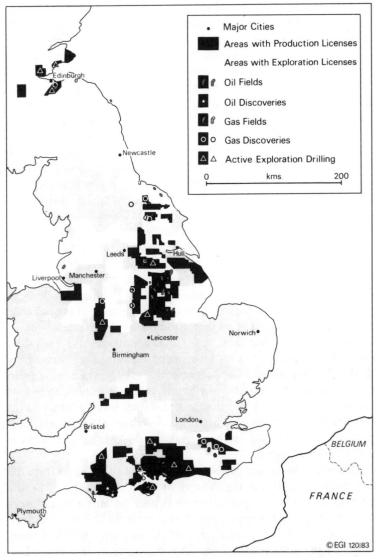

Figure 7.7   On-shore oil and gas fields and exploration/production
concessions

Equally, the large oil and gas entities that are dominant in Britain – either state owned, or the subsidiaries of multinational oil corporations – are neither organised for, nor particularly interested in, small operations. Thus these essentially low-cost oil and gas resources are not being exploited so that the country as a whole, as well as the local communities, fail to benefit from their development.

Meanwhile, at the other 'end' of the oil-producing industry, fiscal considerations are paramount in decision-taking. 'Big' companies and 'big' government struggle over the division of the high levels of economic rent (=supernormal profits) that emerge from the combination of high market prices for oil (and gas) and the essentially low cost attributes of exploiting large oil and gas fields. In the early days of the agreements on production concessions in the North Sea between the oil companies and inexperienced British governments, the latter extended conditions which, for very prolific oil and gas occurrences, proved eminently profitable to the former – particularly as the developments coincided with a period of rapidly rising oil prices. From the 'rip-off' of the early days, however, the pendulum has now swung to the other extreme, and successive governments have enforced concession regulations and fiscal conditions which are essentially counterproductive. These not only absorb the economic rent, but often diminish the real rate-of-return to levels which are unattractive for most oil companies, given their alternative opportunities for investment in many other parts of the world. This has several implications: first, fields which have been developed will be closed down before they are fully depleted, as continued production will not be profitable; second, other fields which have been discovered will not be worth developing; and third, much of the rest of the undiscovered, but discoverable, oil and gas will remain unsought.

This situation has not yet been reached, but the dangers from the too-severe concession regulations and fiscal conditions to the continued effective exploitation of British oil and gas resources remain, in spite of some oil taxation changes in the 1983 budget. Paradoxically, this too-high share of the revenues which is being taken by the government from oil and gas production is used, in part, to subsidise and/or protect the production of inherently higher-cost energy!

Inappropriate Policies

British policy-makers seem to remain convinced that oil and gas are so inherently scarce that any resources found must, *ipso facto*, be so attractive to produce that the main task they face is one of placing restraints on the too-rapid rate of depletion of the resources. Such a view was never correct, except in the period of the temporary politically inspired constraints on oil supplies in the early and late 1970s. It is no longer correct even from the viewpoint of international political considerations, so the prospect now is for some part of Britain's technologically and economically recoverable oil and gas resources to remain unexploited. This, of course, has economic consequences for Britain in the short term, as it means a lower-than-anticipated level of activities in the sector and a diminished flow of revenues and foreign exchange earnings to the government. It is also dangerous to the viability of Britain's longer-term prospects, because it means an unnecessarily high exposure to economic and political pressures from countries which continue to have the opportunity to hold Western Europe dependent on their oil and gas supplies – in circumstances in which the continent's own resources are capable of meeting most of the needs. It is Britain, the best endowed of all the major West European countries with oil and gas resources, that has most to lose from the dangers of inappropriate energy resources exploitation policies – and the most to gain from radical changes in those policies. It is ironic that these important issues, with their contemporary and near-future impact on the country's economy in general, and on the development, in particular, of the regions most closely associated with oil and gas, are given so little attention. By contrast, other energy issues which are of no immediate importance and/or of little significance for at least the next twenty-five years, are accorded a much higher degree of attention. Thus, on the one hand, the unnecessary (and expensive and possibly unsafe) expansion of the country's nuclear electricity generating capacity receives top priority from government energy policy-makers and from the electricity supply industry. This, for Britain, is an issue the consideration of which could be postponed for a decade without any danger to the country's energy prospects.

On the other hand, for other groups the preference appears to lie with proposals for high capital cost and/or unproven alternative technologies, such as the Severn and Morecambe Bay barrages and the geographically dispersed development of wind, water and solar power, etc. Though minor developments of such energy technologies may be justified as pilot projects, their large-scale expansion over the rest of the century would mean an over-commitment of scarce capital resources to the country's now very slowly growing energy sector – at the expense, of course, of the availability of resources for other sectors of the economy and society.

8
Policies for Public Transport

David Banister

Transport is at a crossroads: significant changes in policy have taken place over the last seven years and the future is uncertain, particularly when placed in the context of rising energy prices and recession. The background is well known: growth in the number of private vehicles and in the use of those vehicles. Almost 85 per cent of all vehicular passenger travel is now made by private transport, which has continued to be the main growth area despite a doubling of petrol prices over the last six years. There are two reasons for this. First, petrol prices in real terms are still as cheap as they were in 1975, and second, relative to other modes, the costs of travel by the private car have risen less. Bus travel has declined from the peak levels in 1952 (83 thousand million passenger kilometres) to present level of under half that amount. The rate of decline was stemmed during the 1970s, but recently a significant downturn has taken place, as fares have risen, services have been reduced and levels of revenue support cut. Fewer people travelled by rail in the 1970s but average journey lengths increased. However, in 1979 British Rail were able to reverse this trend through rigorous marketing and fare deals. As many passenger kilometres were travelled in 1979 as in 1962 when the network was some 30 per cent larger. But results for 1982 have shown a reduction due to increases in fares, industrial unrest on the railways and a general economic downturn: these changes are summarised in Table 8.1

Changing Policy Perspectives

The last Labour government undertook the first major review of transport policy since the 1960s with the publication of *Transport*

Table 8.1   Changes in travel patterns and travel expenditure

	1971	1975	1977	1979	1981
Private cars and vans[1]	12,062	13,747	14,050	14,568	15,267
All vehicles[1]	15,478	17,501	17,800	18,625	19,355
Percentage of households with one or more cars	52	56	57	58	61
Private transport use[2]	335	356	381	409	427
Public transport use[2] – road	51	53	49	46	38
– rail[3]	36	35	34	36	35
– air	2.0	2.2	2.1	2.8	2.8
Percentage by private transport[4]	79.0	79.8	81.8	82.8	84.9
Petrol prices (4 star) in pence	35	73	78	117	167
Real price of petrol[5]	80	100	85	86	100
All expenditure on motoring[5]	95	100	100	107	110
Expenditure on bus and coach[5]	102	100	108	115	128
Expenditure on rail[5]	95	100	112	112	117
All public transport expenditure[5] (includes air and others)	102	100	105	106	108

[1] Thousands.
[2] Thousand million passenger kilometres.
[3] Includes British Rail, London Transport, Greater Glasgow PTE and other rail systems.
[4] Percentages include only vehicular transport – walk journeys account for 39% of all movement.
[5] Obtained by deflating the relevant consumer expenditure index by the consumer expenditure index for all goods and services (1975).
Source: GB Department of Transport, 1982.

Policy: A Consultation Document (GB Department of Transport, 1976). Priorities, as seen by the government, were outlined and comments invited. Some 800 representations were made and formed an input to the White Paper on Transport Policy, which crystallised a changed attitude towards transport provision (GB Department of Transport, 1977). The well-established objective of providing an efficient transport system that would contribute to economic growth and higher national prosperity, was supplemented by a social objective 'to meet social needs by securing a reasonable level of personal mobility'. It was explicitly acknowledged that access to opportunities was a high priority and that to achieve this objective both private and public transport services would have to be maintained. Secondary objectives of transport policy included environmental and energy conservation issues.

This social objective marked a change in policy away from continued public expenditure on the motorway and trunk-road network. During the 1960s and 1970s nearly 2,300 kilometres of motorways and 2,500 kilometres of dual-carriageway all-purpose trunk roads had either been constructed or upgraded, and the 'strategic' network was nearly complete. In future, priority was to be given to specific projects, such as the M25 route around London, and it was recognised that transport planning should be more closely related to land-use planning. The assumption of a continued supply of relatively cheap fuel was no longer realistic, and decisions should now be made that integrated land-use functions, so that the 'absolute dependence on transport and the length and number of some of our journeys' could be reduced.

Thus, in the 1978 Transport Act, efficiency and personal mobility feature as the twin objectives of policy; but within the constraints of reduced levels of public expenditure and the conservation of energy, it seemed likely that the success of the second objective would be limited. Events since 1978 have moved rapidly, with a change in government and an unprecedented sequence of transport legislation through Parliament. The first of these was the 1980 Transport Act. Although not explicitly stated, the basic tenets of transport policy have moved towards the provision of transport services at the level and price which the user is willing to pay. Subsidies for public transport services have been reduced and much more opportunity has been permitted for service innovation, including car-sharing and minibus services, and for competition through a relaxation in licensing requirements. The argument is that only through competition and not protection can the user be given the best available service. Consequently it seems that the comprehensive coverage provided by the bus-operator, particularly in rural areas, may be significantly reduced with the end of service cross-subsidisation.

Over the last six years, the level of public expenditure for all forms of transport has declined by nearly 30 per cent (from £6,340 million in 1976–7 to £4,650 million in 1981–2 at 1981 prices). The main cutbacks came under the Labour government in the capital programme, particularly in the rundown of the motorway and trunk-road programme. This approach contrasts with the concern of the Conservative government to reduce levels of current expenditure and even allow a modest increase in the capital programme. It seems that public transport will again come under pressure to cut back services or to further increase fares, while at the same time reducing investment. British Rail may continue to be cushioned from these cutbacks as the public service obligation grant has been raised to £860 million for 1983, and through the provisions of the 1981 Transport Act they will be able to sell shares in any of their subsidiaries and raise investment capital. The Serpell Committee's report (GB Department of Transport, 1983) may change all this. Among their recommendations for improvements in efficiency and productivity, a series of different network options was tested. The most severe of these would result in a network of 2,600 route kilometres, in contrast with the present network of 16,600 route kilometres. It is claimed that this is the largest rail network that would break even; although only 16 per cent of the former coverage, it would carry 43 per cent of existing passenger traffic, but even then it is only with the addition of freight revenue that a small surplus is made. In many ways the Serpell Report reflects the same conclusions that were reached in the famous Beeching Report of twenty years earlier. However, only a financial assessment was made and no consideration has been given to the wider social costs and benefits provided by the rail service.

Finally, the 1983 Transport Act introduces guidelines for public transport subsidies in each of the metropolitan counties and in London. This is an attempt to introduce 'balance and stability' to the financing of public transport after the events of the last two years in London where the 'Fares Fair' campaign has been waged between the Greater London Council and the government. The Act also includes provisions to introduce a three-year rolling plan for operators, scope for the privatisation of services (mainly buffet services) and closer links between government and operators.

So government policy towards public transport has changed in two significant ways. First, public expenditure has been curtailed, particularly on the revenue support side for the bus and coach industry. In real terms, total financial support will be reduced from £457 million in 1975–6 and £242 million to 1984–5, nearly 50 per cent (at 1981 prices). The main reason for this is the disappearance of the new bus grant (Bus and Coach Council, 1982). A similar situation is likely to prevail in the rail sector once the findings of the Serpell Report have been fully discussed. The second change has been the increased control that government has exerted over local transport decisions. The grant system introduced in 1975 was designed to allow a comprehensive approach to transport that examined competing requirements for resources on an equal basis rather than the multitude of specific grants that had existed previously. The primary responsibility for the content of local transport expenditure was to pass from central to local level. The degree of local discretion has been more apparent than real, particularly in the light of this intensive programme of legislation. It is now central government that has financial control over both the amount of grant and allocation of that grant between sectors at the local level, with extensive powers to penalise those local authorities that do not conform to strict centrally determined guidelines.

Changing Patterns of Travel

The changes in transport policy at the national level have been accompanied by alterations in travel patterns and mobility at the personal level. The rate of growth in car-ownership has declined. Perhaps of more interest is the relative stability in the proportion of households with one car (44 per cent in 1971 and 45 per cent in 1981); 15 per cent of households owned more than one car in 1981, although this situation may be influenced by the company-car sector which already accounts for up to 70 per cent of the new-car market.

Prior to 1957, public transport accounted for over half the total vehicular passenger kilometres travelled, but the present level is only 15 per cent, split approximately equally between bus and rail with a small but increasing contribution from air travel. Bicycles have staged a recovery, and walk trips still make up about 39 per cent of all trips, although trip lengths are obviously short. Weekly trip rates now average eighteen per person. With the increases both in trips made and distance travelled there has been a decline in the importance of the work journey to only 18 per cent of all trips. Conversely, shopping and personal business trips and social trips are now responsible for over half all movements (GB Department of Transport, 1982).

Travel patterns are dynamic and are in a continual state of change. Although trip rates and trip distances have increased, the time taken for travel is approximately constant as people are exchanging slower modes (for example, the bus) for faster ones (for example, the car). Clearly the range of activities available is much greater for the car-user than for those using the other modes, and its flexibility and convenience is unparalleled. The overall picture is one of increasing mobility; but for different groups within the population and for different locations the picture is less distinct.

There seem to be three sets of constraints likely to affect individual levels of mobility. They are social, economic, and spatial constraints. For some groups, namely the *young*, social constraints only really apply when they are making unaccompanied trips; they have no physical problem, their problem stems from their limited economic and social independence which may limit mobility. The importance of the bicycle is evident (Table 8.2) 'Housewives' on the other hand often do not have the use of the car during the day as the partner may take it to work. Their activity patterns are often very complex, as their traditional role is to escort children to school, do the shopping and engage in other social activities, and since they may also be in part-time or even full-time employment, their main constraint is time and the problem of scheduling daily activities. The *elderly* often suffer from physical difficulties in movement, but they make nearly half their journeys on foot. They may also experience difficulties in using the bus, particularly in getting on or off, but here again they make nearly 20 per cent of their journeys in this way (Table 8.2). The elderly would perhaps benefit most from the availability of a car, but they are least likely to be in a car-owning household. Working adults have least constraints on their mobility.

Table 8.2   Travel characteristics for selected social groups

Social group	% of journeys by each mode				Journeys per day	Mean journey length (km)
	Car	Walk	Bus	Other*		
Total population	45	35	12	8	2.56	8.1
Working adults	63	21	8	8	3.17	10.8
Young children	323	54	8	6	2.19	5.2
Teenagers	18	48	17	17	2.67	5.6
Elderly	28	47	20	5	1.57	6.3
Housewives	40	47	11	2	2.29	6.5
Low-income adults	25	47	20	8	2.33	6.4

* Includes bicycle, motorcycle and rail.
Source: GB Department of Transport, 1979.

They usually have access to a car and as a consequence make the most journeys, with the longest mean journey length.

Economic constraints relate primarily to income. There is a high correlation between income and car-ownership, and as car-ownership increases so does the quantity of travel. Low-income adults tend to travel less than other working adults (Table 8.2), and the quality of travel is also lower for the poor as they make most of their trips by foot or by bus. Government and local authorities have attempted to reduce the costs of travel for groups at the end of the age spectrum, principally through concessionary fares and school transport. In 1981, £190 million was spent on subsidising concessionary fares on buses (GB Department of Transport, 1982).

Spatial constraints are also important. Residential densities have declined over the last ten years as people have moved out of city centres into urban fringe and rural locations. The net result has been that journey distances have increased. This is particularly evident in rural areas where people have to travel some 30 per cent further than their urban counterparts to reach particular facilities (GB Department of Transport, 1979). However, it may be a mistake to categorise areas as either 'rural' or 'urban'. Many of the problems of transport and accessibility are common to both situations, and levels of mobility relate primarily to car-ownership levels (Figure 8.1).

Although car-ownership levels tend to be higher in rural areas at

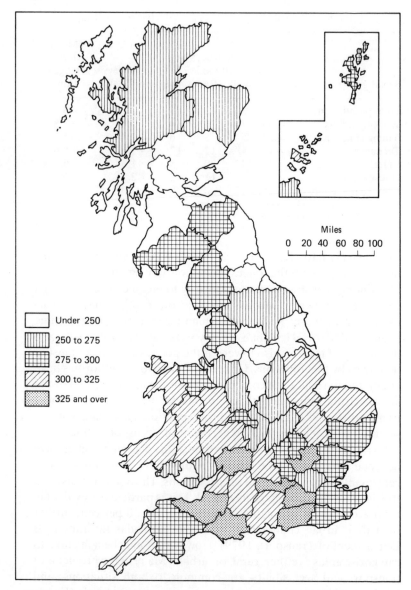

Figure 8.1   Private cars and vans per 1,000 population 1979 by county
Source: GB Department of Transport (1980).

a given income level, the picture presented in Figure 8.1 is more complex. High car-ownership levels are associated with the southern part of Great Britain and in particular with the central southern counties of England. Income levels are some 12 per cent higher than the national average in this region. Conversely, lower-than-average car-ownership levels are found in the industrial centres of Yorkshire and Lancashire, the North East and the central belt in Scotland. Income levels are about 10 per cent lower than the national average in these regions. The expectation would be that remote rural areas would have higher car-ownership levels, but as income levels are lower this is not the case – hence the complexity of the situation presented in Figure 8.1. About 61 per cent of households in Great Britain have the regular use of a car (GB Department of Transport, 1982), but this average ranges from just over 50 per cent in Scotland and the North to over 70 per cent in the South East.

Prospects for Public Transport

Most of the increase in mobility has been within the private not the public sector, as a result of increases in real incomes and the decline in the real costs of motoring. This may be the reason why transport is the only sector within the economy where oil consumption is still increasing. However, with the present recession, the future does not seem to be so predictable. With the increase in unemployment and short-time working there are fewer work journeys, and the reduction in expendable income has also affected recreational and social travel. People are travelling less, particularly by public transport, and some bus companies are cutting back their services by as much as 15 per cent. British Rail have not repeated their good patronage figures of 1979 and announced losses in 1980 and 1982. So the traditional market for public transport has become less important with the contraction in demand for work trips. As these well-defined 'corridors' of movement are ideally suited for public transport, other markets must be opened up.

In the short term, subsidy becomes even more essential to maintain services for those without access to a private car. This includes eighteen million people in non-car-owning households, some 60 per cent of 'housewives' who have no driving licences, many elderly people, and children who are too young to drive. In the longer term a transport policy has to be established. All parties realise that a transport system can only work effectively if there is political commitment to objectives and stability in these objectives. Transport cannot be separated from politics, and intervention has to take place to modify the market mechanisms, particularly to ensure that all people have access to facilities.

With the imposition of strict cash limits on expenditure, certain issues become of crucial importance. Evaluation of public transport has almost exclusively focused on financial assessments of the savings to the operator. The wider community benefits of good-quality public transport have not been measured. Road investment is now evaluated within a much wider framework that includes a full social cost–benefit analysis. Comparability between road, rail and bus investment procedures is necessary so that limited resources can be allocated fairly, both between sectors and within the public transport sector. Some research is in progress on these issues in order that the full community benefits of low-fares policies in urban transport can be evaluated. Investment in public transport infrastructure and new rolling stock has been limited, and certain crucial decisions will have to be made for the railways within the next three years: these include extensive rail electrification, the future of the channel tunnel proposals and the replacement of diesel locomotives. The Serpell Committee's report (GB Department of Transport, 1983) has thrown the debate wide open, and the future of the rail network, at least in its present form, is in doubt. In the absence of comprehensive and comparative evaluation procedures, investment only takes place if the project is considered a national priority (for example, the completion of the M25 orbital motorway around London), or if the funds can be raised from other sources such as the EEC or through private share capital.

The direction that transport is likely to take at this crossroads will be influenced greatly by private initiatives. There may be a basic commercial network for public transport which is operated by both the private and public sectors as a competitive and profitable operation. In addition there will be a social network which will operate as a public service and will be subsidised through national taxes and local rates. The first signs of this change are already apparent with the application by Associated Minibus Operators Limited for a licence to run minibus services on four routes across London, thus breaking London Transport's monopoly on the provision of a public transport network over the whole of the capital. The same might happen to the rail system. The necessity for a transport policy is paramount if these changes take place and a few monopoly suppliers of public transport who provide a service on commercial and social criteria are replaced by a multitude of operators seeking to make a profit. Otherwise public transport as we know it today may disappear by default and not design.

9
Housing in Britain

John R. Short

Housing is an important element in the physical and social fabric of any society. It shelters the population, it is the single biggest non-agricultural land-user, a source of conflict, an arena for political debate and an important sector of the national economy. In this chapter I want to touch upon some of the specific issues in examining three general aspects of housing in Britain: the nature of the housing stock, the operation of the housing market, and the broad outlines of recent housing policies.

The Housing Stock

The housing stock in Britain has been affected by two major changes in recent decades. The first has been the overall improvement in housing quality (see Figure 9.1). This has come about primarily through the slum-clearance programmes of the 1950s and 1960s which swept away whole areas of poor-quality housing. Less important has been the upgrading of existing dwellings through housing improvement.

But against this background of general improvement there are a number of disturbing aspects. There are still households living in overcrowded, poor-quality accommodation. The government's house condition survey of England in 1981, for example, revealed that of 18.1 million dwellings, 1.1 million were unfit for human habitation and 0.9 million lacked basic amenities. The incidence of poor housing conditions is concentrated in inner-city areas. For many residents here it is another strand in a web of multiple deprivation along with restricted employment and educational opportunities which blight the life chances of a significant propor-

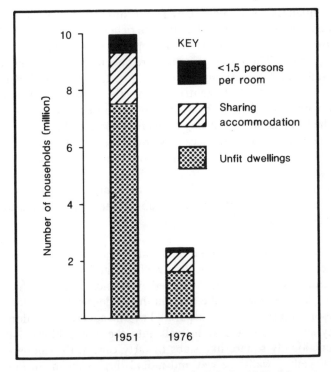

Figure 9.1   Housing quality in Britain, 1951–76

Source: Short (1982b).

tion of the British population. The most recent indicators suggest continued deterioration in the housing stock. Between 1976 and 1981 there was a 22 per cent increase in the number of dwellings requiring more than £7,000 worth of repair (at current prices). In 1981 there were a million such dwellings and a further 2.9 million needed £2,500 worth of repairs. As the slum-clearance programmes have ended and as the recession bites into private and grant-aided improvements, the inexorable deterioration of housing is continuing. Attempts by governments to stop the housing rot have involved the use of improvement grants. Grants to private owners have increased from £66m in 1977–8 to £430m in 1982–3. In the private sector, households can obtain grants which can cover up to 90 per cent of the cost of improvement and repair. While improving the housing stock such a programme has marked redistributional consequences, as public money is put into private hands. All the evidence we have suggests that it is the richer households with older housing who benefit most from improvement and repair grant programmes. Those who gain most are only rarely those in greatest housing need. Often, improvement in certain selected inner-city areas is associated with gentrification – the displacement of older lower-status households by higher-status households.

The local authority housing which replaced the old slums has not proved to be a complete success. Many of the dwellings constructed by industrial systems of buildings in the form of concrete high-rise blocks have created new problems. There are now many estates built in the 1960s which because of damp, condensation and stigmatisation have become the slums of the 1980s. Listen to the voice of despair:

> I have lived in a damp flat on a council estate for two years and have grown cynical of its dwellings and people . . . large gardenless estates drably situated away and apart from the town . . . And here we sit like birds in the wilderness, three flats to a floor, four storeys high, separated by dim concrete corridors and icy stairs . . . it is easy to walk into the wrong block. All are functionally square like slabs of dirty cake with windows. My low-ceiling walls are wet and mould thrives on them. Puddles collect on window-sills. Clothes in the wardrobe rot. (Revell, 1982)

Tenants have voted with their feet and there are now 280,000 local authority dwellings which are officially classified as difficult to let. The ultimate mark of failure has been the demolition of dwellings. In Manchester, Leeds, Liverpool and other British cities the local authorities have literally blown up blocks of housing less than twenty years old.

The second major change in Britain's housing has been the shift in tenure distribution (see Figure 9.2). In both relative and absolute terms private renting has declined and owner-occupation and local authority housing have increased. The contraction of the private rented sector has been caused by the declining rates of relative return afforded to landlords. Investment in private rented accommodation no longer yields the safe and high returns available before 1914. As a succession of Rent Acts has reduced profits and a host

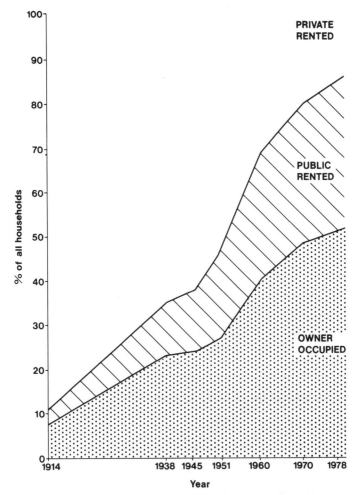

Figure 9.2   Changing tenure distribution, 1914–78

Source: Short (1982b).

of investment opportunities such as building-society deposits have given more profitable, and less troublesome, returns, landlords have sold off their rented properties. Between 1938 and 1976 over 2.6 million dwellings were sold by landlords to owner-occupiers. What remains is a curious mixture. On the one hand there are the very expensive penthouse flats housing the cosmopolitan wealthy, and on the other hand there are the grubby, inner-city bedsits accommodating those unable to afford owner-occupation or obtain a local authority dwelling. Some of the worst housing conditions are found in this latter sector of the urban housing market.

The increase in the number of local authority dwellings is a direct result of political pressure. In Britain the demands have been more strongly articulated after the two world wars, and both post-war eras saw an increase in the number of local authority dwellings. Since it has become such a significant tenure type, the local authority sector has been used from the 1950s onwards as a Keynesian regulator, expanded when reflation of the economy was required, reduced when deflation was desired.

The most significant feature in the British housing market has been the enormous rise in owner-occupation. The majority of British households now own or are buying their accommodation. The expansion of owner-occupation to its position as majority tenure type owes a great deal to rising real incomes, which allow households to afford the cost of purchase, and to government involvement. Through the channelling of subsidies and the exemption from capital gains tax, successive governments have made owner-occupation the obvious tenure choice. Owning a house has been one of the best investments in post-war Britain.

The Operation of the Housing Market

The housing market involves a variety of interests and institutions. Let us examine the main ones involved in the production, consumption and exchange of housing.

The production of housing

Availability of housing is a major constraint in the production of housing. Since 1947, land-use controls have directed the residential development to designated areas. The aim of land-use planning has been to curtail growth. Sprawl has been reduced, but at a cost. The price has been paid in the form of increased land prices, because landowners with land zoned for planning permission can charge higher prices. This has led either to increased house prices or, since there is a limit to the extent to which builders can pass on the land cost to consumers, increasing densities. The consequences have marked social effects. The benefits of planning have been afforded to those living in greenbelt sites, while the costs have been borne by those purchasing relatively cheap new housing. Such buyers have been forced to travel further afield, in effect jumping over the barriers of the greenbelt in order to purchase high-density housing. Availability of land for housing has arisen as an important point of contention. On the one hand builders have sought to get local authorities to release more land for house-building. On the other hand many authorities, especially in high-growth areas, have sought to limit residential development. The balance of power has swung towards the builders as central government has cajoled local authorities to release more land and upheld appeals by builders against local planning authority decisions. In a celebrated case the Department of Environment amended the central Berkshire Structure Plan so that land for an extra 8,000 houses would be released.

The house-building industry is a diverse one. It includes the large-volume builders, for example Barratt and Wimpey, for whom house-building may be only one element in a construction and development empire, to the one-person builder living precariously until the next contract. In the private sector, house-building is a speculative activity in that the houses are produced before being sold. Builders thus rely on external credit because they pay the costs of construction and loan charges before selling the dwelling. Credit bridges the gap between production and consumption. This reliance on extended lines of finance makes the house-building industry particularly sensitive to general business confidence and availability of credit. The decline in private sector starts and completions shown in Table 9.1 demonstrates the point.

In the public housing sector there are two types of house-

Table 9.1   Housing starts and completions in Britain (000's)

	Private sector		Public sector	
	starts	completions	starts	completions
1976	154.2	152.2	170.8	163.0
1981	116.8	114.2	36.9	85.2

Source: Housing and Construction Statistics.

builders: those employed directly by the local authorities – the Direct Labour Organisations (DLOs); and private building firms hired for specific contracts. While the recession has affected the construction sector (Table 9.1 shows the decline in council house building) private builders have mounted a strong attack on DLOs which are direct competitors in a tight market. Conservative central and local authorities have been particularly open to such private-builder lobbying.

Consumption

Housing is expensive. Immediate house-purchase of a dwelling is beyond the reach of all but the wealthiest, and the different forms of tenure can be seen as different solutions to this realisation problem. In the case of owner-occupation, lending institutions advance the purchase price over a twenty- to thirty-year period. In Britain the most important institutions are the building societies, followed by the banks who have increased their market share in recent years, and the local authorities whose lending has declined (see Table 9.2).

Table 9.2   Loans for house purchase in Britain (net advances £million; % distribution in brackets)

	Building societies	Banks	Local authorities	Other	Total
1973	1,999 (69.0)	310 (10.7)	355 (12.2)	229 (7.9)	2,893 (100)
1981	6,331 (64.4)	2,470 (25.1)	252 (2.5)	769 (7.8)	9,822 (100)

Source: Housing and Construction Statistics.

The lending criteria used by these institutions structures the rules of access to this sector of the housing market. As a rule of thumb, the institutions lend two and a half times annual salary with an additional sum for extra wage-earners in the household. A house-hold of two people with one earning £8,000 and one £5,000 is likely to get a mortgage of £25,000 (two and a half times £8,000, plus £5,000). The building societies and banks tend to favour housing built after 1919, standard as opposed to non-standard property, and suburban rather than inner-city locations. These institutions lubricate the process of suburbanisation while doing little to halt inner-city deterioration. The failure of institutions to lend in the inner city, a policy known as 'red-lining', causes uncertainty over property values and discourages property improvement. A vicious circle can emerge as the institutions' refusal to lend causes further deterioration which strengthens the institutions' initial decision not to lend. Red-lining has arisen in the context of a shift in housing policy away from the clearance of older inner-city property. Although local authority mortgage schemes have less strict allocation roles, they are limited in impact, having been reduced in a series of public expenditure reductions, and cannot compensate fully for the other institutions' bias against inner-city areas.

Owner-occupiers purchase not only accommodation but also property rights. In the owner-occupation sector, therefore, households are concerned not only with the utility of the dwelling, its use value, but also its exchange value. Households are therefore particularly sensitive to changes in the local environment – for example, the sighting of a factory, the construction of a new road, etc. – which can affect house prices. A fall in house prices would have a marked effect on their investment. Much of local political activity is concerned with property values as residents act individually and collectively to squeeze the maximum advantage from the constantly changing externality surface which affects property prices. The better-organised, more articulate resident groups are the most successful in reflecting negative externalities. In suburban and rural areas they fight under a number of labels: 'no growth', 'no growth here' and 'not this type of growth here'.

In the case of private renting, the household purchases accommodation through rent payments to a landlord. Some landlords have sought to maintain and improve their profit levels by reducing improvement and maintenance expenditure. The net result has been a steady deterioration in the quality of parts of the private rented sector. Other landlords have concentrated on attracting short-stay tenants – for example, students, young single persons, professional households – whose high turnover allows regular rent increases to be made, and gives the possibility of obtaining vacant possession, a vital factor if the landlord wants to sell property. This emphasis on short-stay households makes it more difficult for households with children seeking long-term accommodation but who are unable to afford owner-occupation or gain access to local authority housing. There is a symbiotic antagonism between landlords and tenants. They both need each other, yet while landlords want to increase profits, tenants want good accommodation at low rents. The precise balance of advantage between tenant and landlord is determined by central government legislation. Throughout the course of this century the balance has been in favour of the tenants, one reason for the lack of investment in the private rented sector.

In the public housing sector the local authority acts as landlord. The housing departments of authorities operate a points system for would-be tenants. Points are gained for different aspects for housing need – for example, large family, poor health, poor quality of existing accommodation. Applicants are then ranked and their names placed on the waiting-list. Housing visitors employed by the housing department interview applicants and grade households on the basis of the interview. This grading is then used to allocate the successful applicants to different types of council housing, with the better-graded households going to the more desirable properties and the poorest-graded households going to the difficult-to-let estates. There have been two associated trends in the local authority housing sector. On the one hand there has been the rise of residents groups. The formation of such groups has been aided by the collective experience of poor housing conditions, expecially in the design failures of the high-rise blocks and in rising rent levels. There has been a variety of community action, some more successful than others. On the other hand many authorities are introducing less paternalistic systems of housing management. Such schemes vary from token participation to the more democratic involvement of tenants. While such schemes tend to incorporate and defuse protest and may be attempts to reduce expenditure by pushing maintenance costs onto the consumer, they can provide the platform for the exercise of greater power by tenants over their housing experience.

Housing is an indication and a reflection of social status. The changing residences of a household act as a series of markers showing progress or regress in the hierarchy of housing consumption, which in the dominant ethos ranges from the local authority high-rise flat to the owner-occupied detached house in the country. Certain types of housing consumption are a symbol of success, others a mark of failure.

The exchange of housing

In the public sector the mobility of households in general is determined by the size of the local authority housing stock, and in particular by the respective housing departments' transfer schemes which match tenants to available vacancies. Mobility within the private rented sector is much easier, involving few bureaucratic or legal transactions; overall mobility is greatest within this sector. In the owner-occupied sector, by contrast, buying and selling involves the exchange professionals: estate agents who introduce buyers to sellers and the solicitors who facilitate the transactions of ownership. The exchange-professionals' fees constitute a significant proportion of the cost of a new house, often amounting to between 3 and 5 per cent of the final price of a house. Such costs, and the hassle and uncertainty involved in the English conveyancing system in particular, tend to work against high levels of mobility. It is difficult and costly to get 'on your bike' even if you are an owner-occupier. At the local level there are many links between the exchange professionals. Solicitors and estate agents, for example, can get mortgages for clients if they channel investment into building societies. In most towns and cities there is a tight network between small building societies, surveying firms and estate agents, all bound by links of overlapping directorships and joint ownership. This cosy little world has provided good living for a minority at the expense of the majority.

The State and Housing

The broad picture of housing policy outputs in postwar Britain is highlighted in Figure 9.3. The main housing policy of successive governments has been the promotion of owner-occupation. This has been the one constant of housing policy over the last twenty-five years, underwritten by a desire to create a large property-owning sector of the population who in turn are respectful of property rights in general. The aim has been achieved through the favourable position afforded to building societies and the money markets, and through generous subsidies. In 1981–2 the typical owner-occupier received an average subsidy of £285 per annum on tax relief on mortgage interests; this compares with the average subsidy of £241

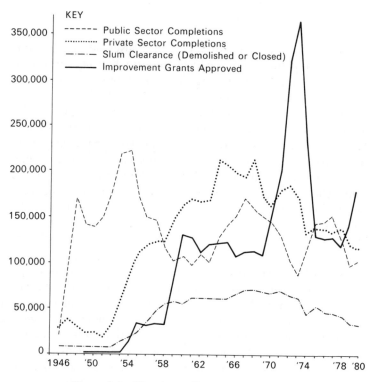

Figure 9.3   Housing policy outputs, 1946–80

Source: Short (1982b).

to the typical local authority tenant. The combined cost of tax relief on mortgage interest and exemption from capital gains tax amounted to £5,060m in 1981–2. This policy has been successful in that owner-occupation is the predominant tenure category and is now the rational tenure choice for most households. But the policy has its costs. Encouragement of owner-occupation has created a vocal interest group sensitive to interest rates. Government expenditure plans are thus constrained by the need to maintain owner-occupier subsidies and to minimise the extent of high interest rates. There is also the more general argument that the preferential treatment given to building societies and owner-occupation has led to a channelling of finance away from other sectors of the economy, notably manufacturing industry. Although the evidence is not conclusive (see Doling, 1982), it is clear that investment in owner-occupation is given preferential treatment compared with investment in job-creation sectors.

The promotion of owner-occupation has as corollary the demotion of local authority housing. This trend has been more pronounced under Conservative governments. Local authority housing has been put in a position of a second-best tenure type, housing those unable to afford owner-occupation. This has been achieved through the sale of council houses and the redirection of housing expenditure. The sale of council houses has been occurring since 1957, but tenants were given a statutory right to buy in the Conservatives' 1980 Housing Act. Since then, almost 125,000 houses have been sold: generally the better-quality ones. Very few flats have been sold. The stock that remains is the poor-quality accommodation which tenants do not want to buy. In a very real sense, then, there is a residualisation as council house sales cream off the best housing. The fostering of owner-occupation and discouragement of local authority housing has also been pursued in government expenditures. While subsidies to owner-occupation have increased, and the raising of the tax relief limit from £25,000 to £30,000 in the 1983 Budget was yet another sign of government openness to owner-occupier demands, local authority subsidies have been decreased. Table 9.3 shows the quite marked decline in

Table 9.3   Public expenditure in Britain (£ million)

	Exchequer subsidies to local authority tenants	Total defence expenditure	Total public expenditure
1977–8	849	6,281	56,789
1982–3	370	14,411	113,007

Source: *The Government's Expenditure Plans 1983–84 to 1985–86*, Cmnd 8789, HMSO.

exchequer subsidies compared with defence spending and total public spending. The most obvious impact of reduced subsidies has been in increased rents, as shown in Table 9.4. The net effect is to force those higher-income households in local authority housing not eligible for rent rebates into owner-occupation. In effect, then, there has been a redirection of housing expenditure. We have to be

Table 9.4   Local authority rents, England and Wales

	Average amount of unrebated rent per dwelling per week (£)	Average amount as % of average weekly earnings
1977–8	5.58	7.1
1982–3	13.55	8.8

Source: *The Government's Expenditure Plans 1983–84 to 1985–86*, Cmnd 8789, HMSO.

careful not to make the mistake of simply seeing these local authority reductions as a drive towards general public expenditure reduction. It has been a restructuring of expenditure to favour owner-occupation at the expense of local authority tenants. How long this will continue is a moot point. The reduction by successive government of housing expenditure is beginning to be felt by lower-income households and is apparent in growing waiting-lists and increasing levels of homelessness. Another housing crisis would seem to be looming.

10
Beleagured Land of Britain

Timothy O'Riordan

From the mid-Victorian period onwards, neither private- nor public-sector-backed developers have been free to alter the quality of life and the attractiveness of the surroundings of the British public without having to account for themselves. In the past this was done through representation during the passage of a private parliamentary bill which enabled individuals, corporations or public bodies to acquire private land (at a fair price) or to run a business (a railway or a power station). Nowadays the private parliamentary bill is more of a rarity, for it is cumbersome and very expensive on both opponents and proponents alike, though it is still used for particularly large projects.

Nowadays the public inquiry normally serves the purpose of permitting debate. But under the planning acts, public inquiries are only mandatory when a planning authority refuses to grant planning permission and the aggrieved applicant formally lodges an appeal. Another possibility is when people whose property and well-being are clearly affected by a proposed development object to an application (these people are known as statutory or second-party objectors). Otherwise the right to hold a public inquiry depends upon the political judgement of the responsible minister, who has wide-ranging powers to 'call in' any matter for determination by informing herself or himself of the relevant facts through a public inquiry. Accountability to the public when environmental interests are damaged is not an automatic procedure nowadays, and usually requires quite a lot of opposition from politically weighty individuals or groups before a public inquiry is held – so long, that is, as the local planning authority and the responsible minister are minded to approve a proposal.

The modern protester over large developments that change the landscape of Britain is less likely to be the second-party or third-party objector. This refers to those who are not directly affected by major schemes (reservoirs, power stations, motorways, for example) – indeed they may live many kilometres from the location of the proposal – but who seek to limit the despoilation of landscapes, the waste of physical resources and the annoyance caused by noise and other forms of pollution that major developments bring in their wake.

Third-party objectors, often dubbed 'environmentalists' in the popular press, can be characterised in a number of different ways. One fairly common division lies between those who dislike certain developments for themselves – for example, motorways, nuclear power stations, radioactive waste disposal – because they do not accept either the purpose or the technology; and those who are not so much opposed to the developments as such but believe that they are not necessary and hence a waste of money. The former group shares values that concentrate on 'soft' technology (based on local materials, maintainable engineering and renewable energy suitable for the human scale), while the latter seek more efficient and frugal use of existing resources (water, energy, wood, minerals).

Another possible subdivision relates to the wish to keep landscapes (both social and wild) exactly as they are, so that they provide a permanent link with past ages, a tangible sense of history, and repositories for wild plant and animal life to exist in their own right and for scientific, educational purposes. This 'museumisation' approach requires careful intervention so as to maintain the cherished features in an artificial state of almost suspended animation. One can contrast this with another group who see in landscapes scope for creating new features – buildings, hedges, ponds and woodlands – which, given careful management, could become the heritage landscapes of tomorrow. The practice of landscape design and enhancement is nothing new – it flourished in Greek and Roman times and was particularly popular in the landscape garden movement of 250 years ago. What is sad is that there is really no modern tradition of imaginative landscape architecture linking the earth sciences to the creative arts. Thus landscape *creators* are a less visible and less co-ordinated breed than landscape *preservationists*, but they share a love of scenic beauty, of the need to bring inspirational beauty into the daily lives of British people, and a dislike of the ugly and the unsuitable.

A latent cause of protest among a minority within both these divisions is a dislike of what is seen as the authoritarian capitalism of the large private and public corporations which promote major investments on the land. Authoritarian capitalism refers to the manner in which well-funded powerful agencies are capable of manipulating business, industrial and government interests to form a common cause of creating capital out of the land, even though its inherent environmental qualities (wildlife, visual beauty, emotional attachment to beloved features in the landscape) are destroyed. Loss of environmental amenity, therefore, becomes part of the wage labour of capital. These institutions not only command influence and money but also expertise. (Examples include the water and electricity authorities, the highway and agriculture departments, the military and major mining corporations.) They can hire the best scientists to undertake environmental assessments, the best engineers to complete the designs, and the best lawyers to promote their case. So the clash is not just one of viewpoint but of power.

This protest is not new: over the past century many battles have been fought between developers and environmentalists. The proposed oil platform construction site at Drumbuie, part of the Scottish coastline held inalienable by the National Trust for Scotland, was subsequently built on a similarly scenic but unprotected coastline at Loch Kishorn a few kilometres away. Today the plant lies idle, barely used and unlikely to be required again. The Cow Green reservoir in Upper Teesdale was never fully used because of industrial recession. The Swincome reservoir on Dartmoor which was never built, and the Aire Valley route in Yorkshire which was never constructed as a motorway, also spring readily in mind.

What is new nowadays is the intensity of the protest (often causing it to break into parliamentary party politics), the growing sophistication and public support for the objecting arguments, the political influence of the opposing coalitions, and the many points of access now available to protesters who seek to change a decision. Since the late 1960s, participation has legally been required in all aspects of planning, so objectors can stall decisions for months and even years simply by manipulating the consultative processes now open to them. The really big development proposals are usually subject to some kind of environmental assessment (EA), known in

North America and Europe as environmental impact assessment. Although EAs are not legally required in Britain, no developer would approach a local planning authority without one, for it is now seen as a means for smoothing the path to obtain planning permission. But the EA may provide information that might not otherwise be known either to the planners or to the objecting parties, and so may open up hitherto unexplored avenues for even more objection and delay. To some second- and third-party objectors, delay through attrition, exploiting consultative procedures for all they are worth and extending public inquiries beyond reasonable length, is part of the game.

The consequence of all this is that site selection for controversial development proposals is a very challenging problem for proponents. As indicated earlier, the three major points of contention are the destruction of loved landscapes and/or natural habitats, the generation of environmental nuisance, and the creation of risk.

Landscape Museumisation and Enhancement

'Landscape' is an emotive term in the British vocabulary. To alter a landscape may not only destroy a tangible link with the past and result in ugliness, but it can also deprive people of a very real part of their sense of place. Nowadays, landscapes are probably changing more rapidly than they did in the past, with the result that fewer and fewer heritage landscapes are left. As preservationists find their backs to the wall they become less willing to compromise (now regarded as a defeat rather than an honourable settlement), so their opposition to change becomes ever more implacable. As attitudes harden, the democratic qualities of decision-making devices such as planning procedures and public inquiries become severely strained.

An example of this occurred in Leicestershire, where many national and local environmental groups combined with two county and four district councils to oppose a plan by the National Coal Board to develop a new coalfield below the Vale of Belvoir. Although the Coal Board had prepared an exhaustive EA of the scheme (reputed to cost over £1 million), indicating how it would minimise landscape change over the life of the development and invest in landscape enhancement afterwards, its arguments did not satisfy the objectors. They were bothered not just about landscape disfigurement but were alarmed at the possibility of miners and their families (even though most would have been from other parts of Leicestershire) together with other industrial workers, entering their neighbourhood: not just as a consequence of the coal development but because of the coal-based chemical industry which they feared would appear in its wake. Though the Coal Board would never admit this possibility, the future of the coal industry is such that it will have to rely on coal-based synthetic fuels for its survival. To date the technology is too expensive but much hinges upon the future availability and price of oil.

After sitting on the inquiry inspector's report for eighteen months, the Environment Secretary chose to ignore his advice, which was to allow the development to proceed with suitable safeguards. Instead he refused the Board's application, but suggested that he would consider favourably a modified proposal which would eliminate the mine in the Vale of Belvoir itself and reduce potential output by 40 per cent. This was a good example of political sensitivity to powerful Tory interests in the East Midlands, though less-charitable observers claim that the decision was also meant to be a warning to the National Union of Mineworkers to control its wage demands and to accept the loss of any expensive and unproductive old pits.

Meanwhile the Coal Board has announced that it is exploring a number of other promising coalfields, most of which are in parts of the country similarly endowed with middle-class respectability, attractive rural vistas and Tory voting strength. The Board will have to proceed very carefully and may again be forced to suboptimise its investments. Likewise, the oil companies seeking to drill exploratory wells in inland England will be confronted with significant protest. Already Shell has suffered opposition to the proposal to drill an exploratory well in the New Forest, with the Nature Conservancy Council, the Countryside Commission and Hampshire County Council making objections at the public inquiry. A ministerial decision is awaited but it would be surprising if the application is successful.

It is worth pointing out that the current economic recession affects both these coal and oil exploration issues in two ways. Industrial decline and more efficient use of energy have combined to lower the demand for energy by over 15 per cent. Tight and expensive money means that investment cash is not readily available. So it may suit a developer to be stalled, and in some cases even a ministerial refusal is currently not such a blow as it might seem.

Agricultural Change and Landscape Protection

The landscape and habitat preservation issue is even more contentious nowadays when major agricultural improvement schemes are proposed. Large-scale drainage schemes or moorland reclamation projects, for example, can alter the visual appearance of vast tracts of land and irreparably alter ecosystems. These schemes are particularly frustrating to environmentalists since they are not normally subject to planning control procedures, so it is much more difficult for protesting groups to demand and obtain a public inquiry. Drainage is a particularly thorny issue, since modern technology prepares marshes, formally thought to be agriculturally 'worthless', for the plough. The trouble is that the Agricultural Departments which grant aid for drainage schemes (50 per cent of the cost for the basic drainage works such as pumps, roads and arterial drains, and up to 37 per cent for field drainage) do not take into account the social costs of altered landscapes and depleted wildlife; nor are the subsidies paid by the general taxpayer to support the price of the crops that will be produced as a result of the scheme, removed from the calculation. In short, drainage schemes are judged on their agricultural and financial merits, not on the suitability of the land or its social value. This distinction illustrates the clash of views between agriculture as an energy- and capital-intensive profit-making industry, and agriculture as environmentally sensitive husbandry, through which requirements for adequate food and the long-term heritage qualities of the land can be accommodated. The trouble is that too many farmers – and especially young farmers – are led to believe that the only sound agriculture is resource- and capital-intensive industrial agriculture. The present tax system, and other financial incentives to agriculture in the form of price supports and improvement grants, simply reinforce this belief.

The Wildlife and Countryside Act of 1981 highlights this dilemma. The Act stipulates that where landowners apply for agricultural capital grants for improvement schemes in areas designated as sites of special scientific interest (or national parks), and find their proposals blocked by authorities who object on the grounds that such schemes would be detrimental to their interests of promoting nature conservation and landscape amenity, then they *must* be compensated by these authorities (usually the Nature Conservancy Council and the National Parks Authorities). In short, the Act unwittingly establishes the principle that certain agricultural grants are a right (when they are actually a privilege), and that the terms of compensation must cover the loss of income forgone, even when the crops that would otherwise have been produced are in expensively funded surplus – surpluses that must be stored or dumped onto the export market at still more cost.

It is likely that the conservation agencies will not have sufficient funds to buy out farmers whose claims can amount to as much as £250 per ha. for twenty years and possibly longer. In one site, for example, a landowner whose 80 ha. are to be retained as high-water-table grazing marsh – still profitable land, but excellent for bird and water-plant life – will be given a payment of £200,000 annually index-linked to the relative changes in livestock and cereal prices. What amounts to a risk-free capital handout during a time of public sector budget cuts and high unemployment, enrages a mystified public which has little concept of the complexities and rigidities of the political economy of modern agriculture.

Such people are angered further when farmers complain bitterly about the 'threat' of a proposed landscape designation. This is the case *vis-à-vis* the commitment by the Nature Conservancy Council to designate 1,000 ha. of wetland in West Sedgemoor in Somerset as a Site of Special Scientific Interest (SSSI). The site is highly prized for its overwintering water fowl, its ground-breeding marshland birds, its flower-rich meadows and the diverse aquatic plant life of its drainage ditches. The county council, the farmers and the local MPs (three of whom are very influential Tories) all favoured a smaller, central core (about 500 ha., about half of which was already owned by the Royal Society for the Protection of Birds). On the best scientific advice, however, the NCC was convinced of the need to designate the larger area. The agricultural interests (both official and local) immediately accused the NCC of petty dictatorship and of being in the hands of zealots. Local farmers (a minority of the affected landowners) burnt effigies of NCC officials – including one of its Chairman, whose appointment was not renewed by the Tory government – and claimed that they would not co-operate with the NCC over financially backed management agreements which are so central to the working of the Act.

This dispute is probably more bitter than it need be, because it is the first test case under the new legislation, because farmers are worried about 'conservation blight' (loss of capital land value due to conservation designation), and because the land is capable of producing arable crops. It will not be the last, nor has it endeared the farmer's image in the public mind. Already the Labour party is talking of extending planning controls to a wide range of agricultural and forestry improvement schemes (without compensation for loss of land value). The farmer's lobbies know only too well that they must keep their members in order if the Act that they were so successful in shaping against repeated attacks by environmentalists is to be retained.

Nuisance and Risk

'Environmental nuisance' is an all-embracing term covering loss of scenic beauty, noise and pollution. Nowadays one of the most disliked ingredients is noise. It is noise and the associated reduction in property values that cause people to defend their rights to peace and quiet against proposals for new or expanded airports or roads. But 'nuisance' is really a generic term to cover a dislike of economic change and new technology, and the institutions and forces that create these changes.

The battle currently being waged in Essex and Hertfordshire over the possible extension of Stansted as a Third London Airport is but a symbol of this protest. Behind the scenes is a serious move to force a fundamental re-evaluation of British air transport policy on the grounds that greater efficiency in controlling aircraft movement and extending existing airports would obviate the need for the Stansted proposal.

There are many who believe that the whole ethos of transport development is misguided and that conflict over proposed schemes is the only way to bring about this rethinking of policy. Similar moves are afoot over motorway proposals, although the momentum is less clearly discernible since many motorway schemes – and conflicts – are divided into small sections.

These battles are not so much arguments about the proper use of land as about the proper course of policy and investment. This is especially true over opposition to risky technologies and processes. 'Risk' is a curious term, with many meanings. Its proper definition is 'the joint probability of a hazardous outcome', and its likelihood of occurrence is usually defined in numbers of deaths per exposed population over a period of time. Nowadays it is more narrowly attributed to extremely unlikely but possibly catastrophic consequences for people who may be unaware of the dangers in which they are placed and who are powerless to defend themselves.

Behind the growing controversy over risk is a fear of the unknown, a dislike of complex and possibly unmanageable technology, a distrust of scientists who appear to be overconfident of their abilities and uncomprehending of the disquiet that is expressed, and a frustration with the democratic means to take decisions about potentially hazardous products and processes.

Nowhere is this more evident than in the controversy over nuclear power. For better or worse, nuclear power is associated in the minds of a significant minority of British people (between 30 per cent and 40 per cent, depending upon how a poll is conducted) with proliferation of nuclear weaponry, with catastrophic engineering failures, and a dread of cancer-causing radiation with all its associations of inevitable but creeping death. So the two main electricity generating boards in Britain – the Central Electricity Generating Board (CEGB) and the South of Scotland Electricity Board (SSEB) – can expect fierce opposition to any proposal to build a nuclear power station. This will particularly be the case if a proposed plant is to be located in a 'greenfield' site – an area devoid of other power stations and industrial development. For in these areas local opposition is in the majority and local planning authorities invariably refuse to grant planning permission. This is in part the reason why the CEGB abandoned its attempts to place a new nuclear station in Cornwall in favour of a third reactor at Hinkley Point near Bridgwater in Somerset, where the Board hopes there will be a more compliant public and local council.

During 1983 there was a major 'set piece' public inquiry into the merits and demerits of Britain's first pressurised water reactor proposed by the CEGB at Sizewell in Suffolk, where there is one existing reactor. The CEGB has admitted (under pressure from objectors) that one of the reasons for choosing the site was the support of the local council and the public (as deduced from privately commissioned market research surveys). It remains at present to be seen whether the inquiry inspector will find in favour of the CEGB, for while the Board has presented a formidable case, an equally formidable opposition case has been prepared.

Fierce opposition from both local and third-party groups can also be expected for any proposal by British Nuclear Fuels or the Atomic Energy Authority to conduct experiments to discover what kinds of rocks and sediments are most suitable for the long-term disposal of highly active radioactive wastes. Threats of civil disobedience against test-drilling geologists are not uncommon. In 1981 the government announced that it was abandoning its test-drilling programme, on the spurious grounds that the necessary research was being conducted in other countries. Its own Radioactive Waste Management Advisory Committee deplored this decision, noting that the vital geological examinations could not be completed abroad. Long-term disposal of the highly active wastes will not occur until the twenty-first century, when attitudes and technologies may have changed, but it seems likely that deep-rock disposal on inland sites may only be permitted on lonely stretches of private land.

Modern land-use conflicts in Britain are fuelled by a number of motives, only one of which is a desire to protect the quality of life. There is a mood in the nation that a different pattern of economic change should be followed and that the omnipresence of environmental quality is an essential part of civilised life. Linked to this mood is a firm belief that environmental assessment should not only be mandatory for all development schemes but that such assessments should encompass the underlying policy as well.

Also associated with this mood is a feeling that the set-piece public inquiry examining a particular proposal on a specific site is no longer appropriate. It is too cumbersome, too loaded down with documentation, too legally formal, too expensive and time-consuming, and too unfair on objecting parties. Without a guarantee of funding underpinned by public subsidy, these groups are unlikely to command the technical and legal expertise to do their arguments justice. In addition, such inquiries do not and cannot satisfactorily debate the merits of government policy which shape the contentious proposals (be it a road, airport or power station). There is a growing belief that major inquiries should be conducted in two stages – both on a small scale – when the site-specific phase is preceded by a debating forum, operating on a more inquisitorial than cross-examining style, which may involve Parliament (probably through one of its select committees but possibly through special commissions).

As protests grow it is likely that developers will look for means of 'buying out' the opposition. In the case of proposals where there is no choice of site – mining and fossil-fuel extraction, for instance – technologies of exploitation will have to be improved to minimise landscape damage. Already there are many promising developments in the understanding and practice of landscape restoration and creation, though more needs to be done.

Where there is a choice of site – for roads, reservoirs, power stations, for example – it is likely that developers will wish to concentrate proposals on sites where damage has already occurred. Hence the preference by the Electricity Boards to cluster nuclear power reactors so as to share transmission lines and local services. This may also be part of the reason why the Boards are prepared to bribe local communities with new sports facilities or community centres to reflect the cost of the extra risk burden they are shouldering on behalf of the nation as a whole.

Land-use conflicts are important to study because they tell us a lot about how people view the world and judge the future. Such conflicts also help to clarify priorities, reshape the distribution of power, and place 'the quality of life' in context. They also reveal the strengths of a pluralistic democratic society: should they ever disappear we should all become concerned.

11
Conflict and Change in the Countryside

Malcolm J. Moseley

It is impossible to say unambiguously which are the truly *rural* areas of Britain. There are plenty of indicators to use, such as land-use, population density, distance from towns, and the degree of economic reliance upon agriculture, but in the end, two conclusions always emerge. First, there are peaks, troughs and gradients of rurality, not clear breakpoints. And second, each indicator tells a confusingly different tale and composite indicators tend to fudge the issue. Nevertheless Figure 11.1 sets out one possible definition, and it is broadly with the characteristics of the areas shown that this chapter is concerned.

The essence of 'rurality' lies in the geographical scatter of people, jobs and services, and this 'dispersed' characteristic underlies two of the chief problems experienced in rural Britain today – 'rural deprivation' and 'landscape deterioration'. But these problems are just part of a much wider picture of rapid change as Table 11.1 makes clear.

Table 11.1   Rural Britain in the 1970s: approximate annual rates of change

	% per annum
Transfer of farmland to urban use	0.1
Decline in agricultural workforce	2
Increase in agricultural output	1.5
Population growth	0.5 to 1.0
Closure of village shops	1 to 3
Closure of sub post offices	1 to 2
Increase of cars owned	2 to 4
Increase of road traffic in rural area	3 to 4
Pleasure craft licensed	4

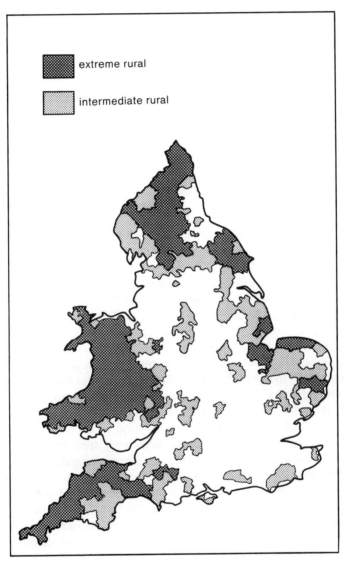

Figure 11.1   Rurality in England and Wales

Source: After Cloke (1977).

Rural Deprivation

'Rural deprivation' is an umbrella term which includes both the difficulties experienced by poorer rural residents in getting to work and to the services they need, and the havoc wreaked upon the provision of services in the countryside by rising car-ownership and by rising economies of scale. The rundown of public transport and the closure of village shops, schools and post offices provide examples. But the problems of rural people go much deeper than this of course. The deprivation suffered by this significant, if inconspicuous and generally inarticulate, rural minority is as closely linked to national developments as to those with a clearly rural dimension. Figure 11.2, for instance, maps the contemporary geography of unemployment: there may be a rural element but it is swamped by the enormity of the national malaise.

The nature of the rural housing problem has changed enormously in the post-war period. No longer is there a serious *physical* housing problem – the absence of piped water, electricity or adequate sewerage, gross overcrowding, dampness and squalor. The problem now is one of *access* to housing, as well-heeled commuters and retired couples compete for what was traditionally working-class housing. In commuter villages (detached suburbia) and second-home villages (seasonal suburbia) the conflict is between those who can buy and those who must rent. With rural council house building traditionally modest in quantity and now at a virtual standstill, there is little that local authorities can do to reserve the expanding housing stock for those who by dint of their employment or family ties may fairly consider themselves as 'local'.

But is what is happening in the retirement areas of Wales, the South West and East Anglia really so different from developments in, say, gentrified Islington? What we see, in fact, is grossly unequal competition in the housing market – a feature of British society as a whole. In short, while the rural element of 'rural deprivation' does exist, as in the accessibility problem and in the attractive environment that lures unwitting retirement migrants to havens that can turn into prisons, its real causes and solutions lie elsewhere.

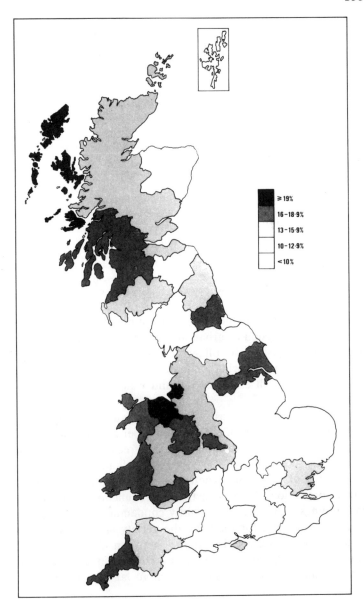

Figure 11.2   Unemployment in Britain, October 1982

Landscape and Land Use

The same is broadly true of landscape deterioration. But before we consider landscape (the *appearance* of the land), the main elements of land-use (the *activities* on the land) need to be spelled out. Table 11.2 sets out the main changes that have taken place over the last forty years.

Table 11.2   The changing land-use of England and Wales, 1939–80 (% of total)

	Rough grazings	Permanent pasture	Arable	Woodland	Urban
1939	14.9	42.3	24.1	6.2	8.6
1961	13.4	29.0	36.7	6.9	9.9
1980	11.4	26.4	36.3	8.0	11.6

Source: Parry (1982) collating Agricultural Statistics and research by R. H. Best.
  Note: Rows do not add to 100% – some land is unaccounted for.

The main elements of land-use change in post-war rural Britain have been the extension of urban areas, the shift from roughland and permanent pasture to tillage, the extension of forest and woodland, and the growing competition for rural land from quasi-urban uses such as recreation and water-gathering (Parry, 1982).

The changes that have most affected the visual landscape have included the steady removal of hedgerows (perhaps one quarter of the total since the war) and of hedgerow trees; the drainage of wetlands; the ploughing up of meadow, moorland and downland; the clearance of deciduous woodland and the spread of single-species afforestation; and the construction of functional and austere farm buildings. All have been rightly condemned for destroying wild-life habitats and for reducing the variety and charm of the landscape, and all reflect the conflict between alternative rural land-uses. But deeper down they express changes in technology, in society's values and in economics, which go far beyond the rural domain.

Conflict and Power

In short, for all its visual tranquility, the British countryside is a battleground of interest groups embodying the divisions and uncertainties of contemporary society as a whole. At one level, there is conflict between neighbouring residents: the car-owners who undermine the bus services of the car-less, and the second-homers who inflate the housing market of the indigenous. At another level there is conflict between decision-makers, such as the Ministry of Agriculture officials who encourage farm modernisation, and their Department of Environment counterparts who promote landscape conservation and who also, via the Development Commission, stimulate employment generation. At a grander level all this expresses a conflict between societal goals such as efficiency, equity and amenity, and, it may be argued, a class struggle between those who own land and capital in rural areas, and those who do not.

In short, in trying to comprehend the rapidly changing rural scene we are forced to examine the locus and exercise of power. And this is not an easy thing to do. It is much simpler to say where real power does *not* lie, namely with any agency having 'rural' or 'countryside' in its title! The Council for Small Industries in Rural Areas, the Rural Community Councils, the Development Board for Rural Wales, the Council for the Protection of Rural England, the Countryside Commission, all intervene usefully to counter aspects of rural deprivation and landscape deterioration, but all are essentially palliative. Even statutory local authority planners, with legal powers to devise, and supposedly enforce, land-use plans, are humbled by an economy with 12 per cent unemployment, an agricultural industry immune from most of their powers, and by national and regional resource agencies (notably for agriculture, forestry and water) similarly outside their jurisdiction. It is really rather odd that students of the rural settlement pattern, for instance, have lavished so much attention on the planners and their plans and so little on the massive spending authorities such as the Post Office, the Regional Water Authorities and the county council education committees.

But it would be wrong to pretend that it is the big battalions in the public sector that wield all the power. Another aberration in the development of rural geography has been its naïve ignorance of land-ownership. Only in a romantic sense does the countryside 'belong to the nation'. Ministry of Agriculture figures indicate that the agricultural part of it belongs to owner-occupier farmers (55 per cent), to private landlords and trusts who let it to tenant farmers (a further third) and to a variety of public and semi-public bodies. Financial institutions own a small (less than 2 per cent), but growing, proportion.

The point is that by any standards British farmers and landowners are a privileged group. First, they are massively subsidised: in her 1981 book, *The Theft of the Countryside*, Marion Shoard estimates that through direct cash grants and guaranteed prices, British farmers received more than £1,000,000,000 from the Common Agricultural Policy of the EEC in 1980. And they enjoy exemptions from local pressure that are unique in the world of industry and commerce. Not only are the businesses exempt from local taxes, but they can uproot Saxon hedgerows, erect farm buildings and turn meadows into arable prairie, without informing, let alone seeking permission from, the local authority. No businessman in the manufacturing or service sector enjoys such a *carte blanche* to pursue selfish interests. The fact that many farmers are benign custodians of their landscape rather than profit maximisers is neither here nor there. The principle that society should be empowered to curb without compensation environmentally detrimental business activity, should apply to the landscape as much as it does to the townscape.

Moreover, farmers and landowners are often the 'gate-keepers' of rural society. Research in East Anglia by Essex University sociologists has revealed their dominance in local politics which, when coupled with their strategic position as employers, housing landlords, magistrates, etc., amounts to a considerable concentration of power in a few hands. And, perhaps most important of all, British farmers enjoy the fruits of what Wibberley has called 'the curse of agricultural fundamentalism' – an uncritical popular belief that 'farming as an occupation is next to godliness' and that whatever the farmers do is in the long-term interests of society.

Looking Ahead

How will Britain's rural areas develop over the rest of this century?

Much will depend on the expression of changing attitudes and philosophies. Who could have anticipated twenty years ago, in the heyday of the tower block, the new town and the urban motorway, that there would be massive shifts from comprehensive redevelopment to gradual rehabilitation, and from decentralisation to an 'inner-city' policy which would reassess the whole direction of urban planning? Similarly, it is difficult now to forecast the major shifts of opinion which could transform rural Britain.

But much will surely depend on the changing definition of the rights and responsibilities of the state, the market and the individual. The contentious issue of farmers' rights to do what they will with the land has already been mentioned. As far as rural deprivation is concerned, one scenario might be the progressive withdrawal of subsidies to rural service provision as part of an 'on your head be it' policy for rural life. This would accelerate the demise of rural bus services and schools, and require highly optimistic assumptions about the ability of 'the community' to plug the gaps. There has certainly been an upsurge of volunteer-based initiatives in recent years, from community buses to bulk-buy co-operatives, but it is hard to see such schemes ever being comprehensive in their coverage.

Another unknown relates to the scope for better co-ordination of government policies in what will always be the 'residual' areas of a largely urban nation. Would the countryside be better served if instead of sectoral programmes aimed at the whole of rural Britain, we had comprehensive programmes aimed at particular rural areas? These could be analogous, perhaps, to the inner-city partnership schemes which have sought to wed a disparate set of public agencies to a common purse and set of local objectives.

Perhaps the future of rural Britain will depend on how far people will opt for the 'package-deal' of rural life and choose to live there and invest there. Here there is fascinating scope for speculation. Many American commentators, looking at the latest population trends in their country, posit a 'clean break' with the long history of steady urbanisation that has characterised nineteenth- and twentieth-century America. There, it is the rural areas, irrespective of their proximity to the big towns, that grew fastest in the 1970s. This is ascribed to a 'post-industrial economy' in which the availability of communications, rather than transport, and of an attractive environment, dictate the location of new employment.

Wedded to this is a re-thinking of traditional values, with the 'good life' of the sun-belt taking precedence over the 'rat-race' of the industrial cities.

Recent British evidence points in the same direction. Between 1971 and 1981 the total population of Great Britain stood virtually static at 54 million. But this masked enormous local variation (Table 11.3). *All* the metropolitan counties experienced massive out-migration. And throughout rural Britain, except in isolated pockets and the remotest upland areas, the population grew, often substantially (Figure 11.3).

Table 11.3   Population change, 1971–81

Inner London	−18%
Outer London	−5%
Main cities of the metropolitan counties	−10%
Large towns (over 175,000)	−5%
Smaller towns	−3%
Mixed urban–rural districts	+8%
Remoter, largely rural districts	+10%

Source: Census, Report (1981) *Preliminary Report: England and Wales*, Office of Population Census and Surveys, London.
Note: The definition of the geographical categories is complex, but the overall pattern is clear.

Together with residential preferences and the geography of the post-industrial economy, it is the pattern of state expenditure which will dictate the future scale of economic activity in rural Britain. And in this respect Table 11.4 suggests how myopic it is to

Table 11.4   Financial transfers 1978–9

Rate support grant paid to non-metropolitan England and Wales	£4,106,000,000
National grants and subsidies to British agriculture	£240,000,000
Support to British agriculture under CAP market intervention	£330,000,000
Highland and Islands Development Board income	£16,000,000
Development Commission income	£16,000,000
(of which to CoSIRA)	£8,000,000
Development Board for Rural Wales income	£7,000,000

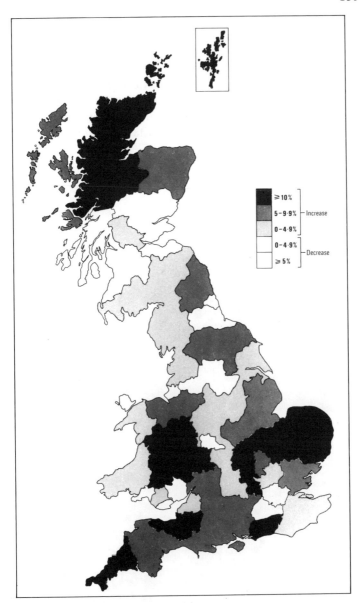

Figure 11.3   Population change, 1971–81

concentrate attention on localised industrial subsidies. A one per cent change in the total size, or the urban/rural allocation, of the Rate Support Grant (RSG), far outweighs the entire budget of the Development Commission and similar rural development agencies. And RSG means jobs, as well as services, as any redundant school-dinner lady will affirm. The scale and use made of massive transfer payments by the British and European authorities will in large part fashion the way that rural Britain develops. And that brings us back to the exercise of power.

12
The Geography of Intervention

Peter Hall

The geography of contemporary Britain is one of rapid and unpredictable change. That was probably true at any period in the last fifty years – or the last hundred and fifty. What is new, and disconcerting, is the feeling among many informed people that it is going to be very difficult to do anything about it; and further, that anything that could be done would be so drastic that many people would reject it. That, perhaps, only reflects the increasing political polarisation of British society in recent years. But that in turn only reflects the intractability of the problems with which politicians, and their professional planners, have to grapple.

The most important of the changes can be simply stated. It is nothing less than a new map of growth and decline – a map that is almost the obverse of the map of a hundred years ago, and that is drastically different from the map of even twenty years ago. A century ago, the map of population change would show dark smudges around all the major cities, representing the rapid industrialisation and spread of what Patrick Geddes, in 1915, was to christen the 'conurbations'. Conversely, great tracts of rural England – East Anglia, the South West Peninsula, the East Midlands – and of Middle and North Wales were areas of population outflow, as people left ruined farms for the cities. Twenty years ago, suburbanisation was already lapping far out from the conurbations into the Home Counties around London, into rural Warwickshire and Worcestershire, and into North Cheshire.

But now, the map of population change in the 1970s, between the censuses of 1971 and 1981, shows all Britain's major urban areas as zones of decline and decay, while the most dynamic parts of the country are the rural peripheries. Against a background of negligible growth in the country as a whole – a growth for the entire

United Kingdom of only 170,000 for the whole decade – Greater London lost 10.1 per cent of its population, or over 750,000; Merseyside lost 8.6 per cent, Tyne and Wear 5.6 per cent, the West Midlands 5.3 per cent, Greater Manchester 4.9 per cent, South Yorkshire 1.6 per cent and West Yorkshire 1.5 per cent. And within these figures for the metropolitan counties, Manchester lost 17 per cent, Liverpool 16 per cent, Newcastle 10 per cent, Birmingham 8 per cent and Sheffield 6 per cent. Not only the big conurbations, but many of the larger freestanding cities like Bristol, Hull, Leicester, Nottingham, Derby, Stoke-on-Trent, Cardiff, Swansea, Southampton and Portsmouth are also losing. Most of these, admittedly, have growth outside their boundaries.

The cores of urban Britain were thus decaying, while the rural peripheries surged. Those counties with the fastest rates of growth included Cambridgeshire, Norfolk and Suffolk in East Anglia, and adjacent Northamptonshire in the East Midlands; Somerset and Cornwall in the South West; Shropshire and Powys in the Welsh Marches. Within the South East, not long ago the most dynamic region of Britain but now losing people overall, only two counties showed big gains: Sussex, which experienced both retirement migration and the impact of the Crawley–Gatwick growth zone, and Buckinghamshire, while Milton Keynes was the fastest-growing single local authority area in Britain.

In other words, Britain now seems to be experiencing a close parallel to the trend much observed recently in the United States, of a movement away from the urban areas and into the rural (in American parlance, the 'nonmetropolitan') periphery. Some of the gains in the rural counties, as in Shropshire and Northamptonshire and Cambridgeshire, represent new-town development. But elsewhere, there seems little doubt that the movement is now into genuinely rural areas, outside the commuting spheres of the bigger cities.

The question must be whether anything much can be done about this – and whether enough people want to do anything about it. True, the Labour government of James Callaghan wanted to do something about the decline of the inner cities, and passed an Inner Urban Areas Act (in 1978) to try to stem it. The partnership areas in seven conurbation cities, the programme areas in more than a dozen others, were the result. The Conservative government of

Margaret Thatcher has maintained the broad thrust of these policies and has supplemented them with urban development corporations for the London and Liverpool docklands, plus enterprise zone designations for eleven badly decayed urban areas, supplemented in 1982 by eleven more.

Judgement on all these initiatives is still far too early, but meanwhile the population loss has continued – and so has the job loss which is the source of it. Careful research by a number of geographers and urbanists reaches broadly the same conclusions in London, in Manchester and in Glasgow: that job losses mainly result from complete plant closures unaccompanied by new plant openings; the inner cities have lost their historic roles as incubators of new enterprise. Whatever dynanism the British economy has, it is no longer to be found here. And that leaves millions of people, in particular the younger unskilled workers and the older blue-collar workers whose plants have closed, without a job – and without much prospect of one either.

That pattern is even true in the still-growing service or tertiary sector of the economy. Only London shows much dynamism here; the provincial cities are not holding their own as office centres. And in London, the politics of intervention demonstrate curious contradictions, as Labour borough councils (such as Southwark) bless large-scale office developments while others (such as Lambeth) do their utmost to stop them in conjunction with a Labour GLC. But the message from Marsham Street to County Hall is now clear: London will get office development, through the Docklands development corporation, whether County Hall likes it or not. Against that, local authorities that exceed Marsham Street's concept of reasonable spending will be penalised – and they tend to be the big inner-city authorities.

Outside the decaying conurbations, also, the new politics of intervention have been clearly delineated by Michael Heseltine as Secretary for Environment between 1979 and 1983. Structure Plans are to make adequate allowance for industrial and commercial development. They are also to ensure that enough housing land is available for five years' needs. To provide the necessary resources against a background of public expenditure cuts, the rate support grant has been shifted to favour the shire counties. Further, the new-towns programme is going ahead – albeit on a reduced scale, and with many of them regarded as effectively completed – and the major growth areas in South East England, relic of the 1970 regional plan and of an age of expansion, remain in force.

In other words, the geography of intervention is currently, and in large measure, a geography of reinforcing the trends. Industrial development certificates, once the basis of regional policy, are effectively dead. Regional incentives, in contrast to five years ago when they were available in half the country, are now restricted to the urban disaster areas. The effective policy is: Britain needs growth wherever it happens – and it happens in the small towns with good amenity and the right basis for attracting key workers into high-technology industry and growth services.

This will be maximally unpopular with the Labour party, whose voting base is concentrated in the eroding areas of the country. It may be unpopular with some Conservatives, who want to preserve their rural bailiwicks just the way they are – and Heseltine and his successors did pay some lip-service to that, with his emphasis on urban and rural conservation for those areas worth conserving. But on the other hand, it may be the only kind of policy left when all other regional and urban policies seem near-bankrupt. And it does have some support from the experience of the United States, where in the last thirty years just such high-amenity areas, in the Sunbelt states of the south and west, have boomed on the basis of new industries, while the traditional nineteenth-century industrial cities have decayed. The critical difference is that America's Sunbelt is very big and is adding millions of new jobs, while Britain's Sunbelt (if that is the right term) is, in relation to the total size of the country, miniscule.

It is, however, going to be a hard policy to sell. Almost universal experience suggests that mature and fairly affluent societies become intensely conservative in their attitudes towards preserving the environment. Britain was already committed to that conservatism in the 1950s; since then the mood has been exported to the plushier and more highly developed parts of the American Sunbelt, notably to northern California. It is no accident that San Francisco was the first American city (and perhaps the first in the world) to abandon freeway building, in 1959; or that the San Francisco Bay Area was the first to follow Britain in trying systematically to contain the growth of its urban areas. For it merely reflects that at a certain point the politics of redistribution of real income create – as the American economist Lester Thurow puts it – a 'zero sum society', in which gains to one group mean losses to another.

The tendency, in such a situation, is for the existing occupiers to protect their position against the threat of change. So, in general, no power stations, no major public housing, no (or very few) motor-ways, no new airports. But of course many of the pressures for change will inevitably occur just where these well-heeled defenders of the status quo happen to live: in the rural interstices between the major urban areas, where much of the maximum pressure for growth happens to be taking place. It is no accident that the M25 around London and the M42 south of Birmingham were two of the most embattled motorways in all Britain, or that locating a new airport to serve London should have been a subject of bitter controversy for nearly twenty-years without result so far.

Some, of course, would use this opportunity to say that this is where positive, even draconian planning makes its comeback. Such a policy, it is argued, could achieve that rarest of outcomes: a move to a Pareto-optimal position, where not just one but many people are better off than before, while none are worse off. If we poured resources into the decaying cities and into the declining parts of the United Kingdom (such as Scotland), the people in these regions would have the chance of good and secure jobs and higher incomes, while the threat of destruction of environment – so poignantly put by Colin Buchanan in his attack on the Stansted airport proposal – could be lifted.

The problem about this policy, in present circumstances, is that it would involve the use of powers so great as to be almost unimaginable, and with a totally uncertain outcome. It would be necessary to direct industry to the decaying cities and areas, and to place a stop on development in growing ones. But there is very little mobile industry now, in contrast to the 1960s when there was plenty; so the policy would involve actually throttling new enter-prise, or such as there is of it in Britain nowadays, at birth. Further, because the remaining mobile industry mainly represents invest-ment by the multinationals, it would be necessary to bring them also under some kind of control, of a kind that is sometimes hinted at, but never clearly stated.

It would also mean starving the growth areas of the infrastructure, whether in the form of roads or sewers or schools or hospitals, there are needed to provide adequate service for the new people. In practice no British government since 1950 – that is, no British government in ordinary peacetime conditions – has done that; and despite likely protests to the contrary from sections of the Labour party, it is extremely unlikely that in practice any future government would do so either. So the best bet is that the trends of deconcentration and of counter-urbanisation (or better, counter-conurbanisation) will continue, that public intervention will continue also either to back them or weakly to acquiesce in them, that the result will be plenty of controversy and not a little blocking action: in other words, more of the history of the last three decades.

What, then, would be the likely resulting geography of the 1990s? Bear in mind, first, that the re-election of the Thatcher government rules out any radical alternative economic strategy – particularly if the threatened abolition of the GLC and the metropolitan counties removes any possibility of local economic initiatives from that quarter. Therefore, for almost the whole of the 1980s we can be sure of a continuation of the relative non-interventionism of 1979–83. The results, we can say with some confidence, are likely to be as follows.

First, the decline of the inner cities will not be arrested. The Enterprise Zones and the Urban Development Corporations and the Urban Development Grants may together attract private capital into some areas – for instance, the London Docklands; but for every one of these initiatives that bears real fruit, there are likely to be five or six others that are relatively unsuccessful in the central task of generating new firms, new productive plants and new jobs. (Movements across boundary lines, to take advantage of generous incentives, are another matter; but they will have no net effect on the inner-city problems as a whole.) The successes are likely to be in those cities that have some continuing locational advantages for certain activities – above all, London, as a centre for high-level national and international offices. The failures are likely to be in the inner cities of the peripheral regions.

Second, despite well-organised opposition and consequent delay, major infrastructural investments will be completed in the outer city regions and interstitial zones. The M25 London Orbital is virtually certain to be completed by 1986; the M42 West Midlands Orbital at about the same time; the M3 from London to Southampton by the late 1980s; and (more problematically) the M40 from Oxford to Birmingham at about the same time. The Third London Airport will be started, whether at Stansted or in the form of a Fifth Terminal at Heathrow; and, whichever is the case, the effect will be to attract industry and warehousing farther out. Thus, ironically, though the 1970 Strategic Plan for the South East can be regarded officially as dead, its essential spirit – the development of a vast polycentric city region in South East England, tied together by the M25 and the connecting radial motorways – is likely to be very much alive.

Within this region, and just beyond its borders, certain zones are likely to show especially vigorous growth: the high-technology areas of the M4 Corridor from London to Bristol, the Milton Keynes region, the Cambridge region. In several of these, there will be weak protests against the resultant pressures for residential building but relatively little opposition to job generation, especially since much of it will take a sympathetic form in R & D laboratories and 'clean' factories. Where counter-pressures are successful, they will divert growth locally, not out of the area altogether; thus Cambridge to Haverhill, Harlow or Peterborough, Bracknell to Swindon. And a further generation of highway infrastructure – as already suggested for the late 1980s and 1990s in the 1970 Plan – will reinforce these patterns, by enhancing the connections between the cities and towns at the periphery of the region.

The resulting geography of Britain at the end of the twentieth century is likely to bear a strange resemblance to that of the fourteenth. It will almost be as if the first industrial revolution was an unhappy accident of history, whereby – by some misfortune – an agrarian settlement structure of smallish, evenly-spaced towns was supplanted by new industrial colonies forcibly located on the coalfields. Other European countries, where the process of industrialisation came later, did not experience this phenomenon to nearly the same degree; and there too, in Belgium and in Germany, the nineteenth-century industrial cities are in decline and the medieval pattern is reasserting itself. Ironically, the process confirms the foresight of visionaries like Patrick Geddes and Peter Kropotkin, who at the outset of the twentieth century foresaw the liberation of 'Neotechnic' industry from the constraints of coal and steel. Politicians may try to restrain the process in the interests of the now fast-declining industrial proletariat of the nineteenth-century regions; but, on the basis of the General Election of 1983, that political force is approaching extinction. The 1980s may prove to be the decade when, after a half-century of agonised transition, Neotechnic Britain finally came into its own.

Notes on Contributors

David Banister is Lecturer in Transport Policy at University College London. Prior to this appointment he carried out a Ph.D. research programme at the Institute for Transport Studies at Leeds University and he has been a Lecturer in Geography at the University of Reading. He has published three books: *Transport Mobility and Deprivation in Inter Urban Areas* (1980), *Transport and Public Policy Planning* (1980), and *Rural Transport and Planning* (1982).

Bob Bennett is currently Lecturer in Geography at the University of Cambridge, and Fellow, Tutor and Director of Studies in Geography at Fitzwilliam College. His books include *Environmental Systems* (1978, with R. Chorley), *Spatial Time Series* (1979), *Geography of Public Finance* (1980), *Central Grants to Local Governments* (1982), and as co-editor *Towards the Dynamic Analysis of Spatial Systems* (1978), *Quantitative Geography* (1981), and as editor *European Progress in Spatial Analysis* (1981). He is Editor of *Environment and Planning C: Government and Policy*.

John Goddard is Professor of Geography and the Director of the Centre for Urban and Regional Development Studies at the University of Newcastle upon Tyne. He is author of *Office Location and Urban and Regional Development* (1975), and co-author of *British Cities: Analysis of Urban Change* (1982) and *The Urban and Regional Transformation of Britain* (1983).

Peter Hall is Professor of Geography at the University of Reading. He is a regular contributor to *New Society*, and he is author or co-author of *The Containment of Urban England* (1973), *Urban and Regional Planning* (1975), *Great Planning Disasters* (1980), and *Growth Centres in the European Urban System* (1980).

Ron Johnston is Professor of Geography at the University of Sheffield. Political geography is one of his main research interests and he has published widely in the field of electoral studies. Among his many books are *Geography and the State* (1982), *Geography of Elections* (1979, with P. Taylor), *City and Society* (1980), *Political, Electoral and Spatial Systems* (1979), *Philosophy and Human Geography* (1983).

David Keeble is Lecturer in Geography at Cambridge University, and Fellow and Tutor of St. Catharine's College, Cambridge. He is the author or co-author of *Industrial Location and Planning in the United Kingdom* (1976), *Regional Development in Britain* (1980), and *Centrality, Peripherality and EEC Regional Development* (1982).

Andrew Kirby is currently Assistant Professor in Geography at the University of Colorado, Boulder. He has also been Lecturer in Geography at the University of Reading. His publications include *The Inner City, Causes and Effects* (1978), *Education, Health and Housing* (1979), *The Politics of Location* (1982), and *A Public City* (1984); he has also co-edited *Resources and Planning* (1979) and *Public Provision and Urban Development* (1983). He is on the Editorial Board of *Cities* and is Review Editor of *Political Geography Quarterly*.

Paul Knox is Senior Lecturer in Geography at the University of Dundee. He is author of *Urban Social Geography* (1982), and (with Brian Coates and Ron Johnston) *Geography and Inequality* (1977).

Malcolm J. Moseley is Reader in Environmental Sciences at the University of East Anglia. He has published various books and articles on the social and economic development of rural East Anglia and of rural and urban France. He is the author of *Accessibility: the Rural Challenge* (1979).

Peter Odell is Director of the Centre for International Energy Studies and Professor in Energy Studies at Erasmus University in Rotterdam. He is the author of *Oil: The New Commanding Height* (1966), *Natural Gas in Western Europe: A Case Study in the Economic Geography of Energy Resources* (1969), *The North Sea Oil Province* (1975, with K. E. Rosing), *The West European Energy Economy: The Case for Self-Sufficiency* (1976), *The Optimal Development of North Sea Oilfields* (1977, with K. E. Rosing), *Energy Needs and Resources* (1977), *The Pressures of Oil: A Strategy for World Economic Revival* (1978, with L. Vallenilla), *British Oil Policy: a Radical Alternative* (1980), *The Future of Oil* (1980, with K. E. Rosing).

Timothy O'Riordan is a Professor at the School of Environmental Sciences, University of East Anglia. He has written many articles on environmental issues and is author of *Environmentalism* (1981), and with R. K. Turner has co-edited *An Annotated Reader in Environmental Planning and Management* (1983).

John R. Short is Lecturer in Human Geography at the University of Reading. His main publications include *Housing and Residential Structure* (1980, with K. Bassett), *Urban Data Sources* (1980), *An Introduc-*

tion to Political Geography (1982), *Housing in Britain* (1982), *An Introduction to Urban Geography* (1984), and *The Urban Arena* (1984).

Peter Taylor is Senior Lecturer in Geography and Associate Director of the Centre for Urban and Regional Development Studies at the University of Newcastle upon Tyne. His main publications include *Geography of Elections* (1979, with R. J. Johnston), *Seats, Votes and the Spatial Organization of Elections* (1979), and *Section and Party* (1981). He is also co-editor of *Political Studies from Spatial Perspectives* (1981), and editor of *Political Geography Quarterly*.

Guide to Further Reading

1 Britain in Transition (Short and Kirby)

As general background, see Short (1984) and Kirby (1982). Donnison and Soto (1980) provide a useful introduction to the new emerging spatial structure of contemporary Britain.

2 The Geography of the British State (Taylor and Johnston)

An interest in the state has developed only recently among political geographers, and so it is reflected in only a few contemporary texts, including Short (1982b), Johnston (1982), Burnett and Taylor (1981). In their work, geographers draw heavily on the publications of other social scientists: see, for example, O'Connor (1973) and Jessop (1982). For recent treatments of the political geography of the United Kingdom, see Taylor (1983) and Johnston (1979).

3 Industrial Location and Regional Development (Keeble)

General introductions to this theme include Dicken (1982), Fothergill and Gudgin (1982), Hoare (1983), Law (1981) and Manners *et al*. (1980).

4 Changes in the Urban System (Goddard)

See Hall *et al*. (1973) for an early study, and Spence (1982) for more recent work.

5 The Geography of Public Finance (Bennett)

Introduction to and analyses of local government finance in Britain include Bennett (1980, 1982) and Burgess and Travers (1980). More general accounts of the redistributional consequences of state actions include Johnston (1979, 1982) and Smith (1974, 1977, 1979).

6 Public Provision and Quality of Life (Knox and Kirby)

On provision of health, see Black (1982) and Knox (1979), Kirby (1982a) for a discussion of education provision. More general considerations are available in Kirby (1982b) and Knox (1982b).

7 Energy Issues (Odell)

Examinations of energy issues in a British context include Leach *et al*. (1979), Manners (1981), Odell (1979) and PEP (1976). Works on specific energy issues include Addinall and Ellington (1982), Patterson (1977) and Spooner (1980).

8   Policies for Public Transport (Banister)

On questions of accessibility, see Banister (1983) and Moseley (1979). Starkie (1982) and Wells (1979) discuss roads and transport planning, while Nash (1982) discusses the economics of public transport and Hibbs (1982) raises the question of a free-market approach to transport provision.

9   Housing in Britain (Short)

For general books on housing, see Lansley (1979), Merrett (1979, 1982) and Short (1982a). The Department of the Environment provides a useful empirical source in its regular *Housing and Construction Statistics*. The best single source of up-to-date information is the monthly journal *Roof.*

10   Beleagured Land of Britain (O'Riordan)

For studies of the modern environmental movement, see O'Riordan (1981), Sandbach (1980) and Cotgrove (1982). On the countryside conflicts, see various issues of *ECOS* (Journal of the British Association of Nature Conservationists, available from the Department of Landscape Architecture, University of Sheffield), Shoard (1981) and Mabey (1981). On risk matters, see Fischhoff *et al.* (1982). On the nuclear issue, read Stott and Taylor (1981) and Ince (1982). On the public inquiry debate, see Outer Circle Policy Unit (1979) and Macrory (1981).

11   Conflict and Change in the Countryside (Moseley)

Good overviews of contemporary rural Britain are provided by Newby (1979) and Shaw (1979), and in some of the papers in Johnston and Doornkamp (1982). For more specific issues, see Cloke (1977), Dunn *et al.* (1981), Shoard (1981) and Woollett (1981).

12   The Geography of Intervention (Hall)

For the relation between economics and spatial organization, see Hall (1981). More specific discussions are located in Johnston and Doornkamp (1982).

Bibliography

Addinall, E. and H. Ellington (1982) *Nuclear Power in Perspective*, Kogan Page, London.

Banister, D. J. (1983) 'Transport and accessibility', in M. Pacione (ed.), *Progress in Rural Geography*, Croom Helm, London.

Bennett, R. J. (1980) *The Geography of Public Finance: Welfare under Fiscal Federalism and Local Government Finance*, Methuen, London.

Bennett, R. J. (1982) *Central grants to local government: The Political and Economic Impacts of the Rate Support Grant in England and Wales*, Cambridge University Press, Cambridge.

Black, Sir D. (1982) *Inequalities in Health* (The Black Report), Penguin, Harmondsworth.

Bunge, W. (1982) *The Nuclear War Atlas*, Society for Human Exploration. Arthabaska, Quebec.

Burgess, T. and T. Travers (1980) *Ten Billion Pounds: Whitehall's Takeover of the Town Halls*, Grant McIntyre, London.

Burnett, A. D. and P. J. Taylor (eds) (1981) *Political Studies from Spatial Perspectives*, Wiley, Chichester.

Bus and Coach Council (1982) *The Future of the Bus*, A Special Report from the Bus and Coach Council, London.

Butler, J. R. and R. Knight (1974) *The Designated Areas Project Study of Medical Practice Areas*, Health Service Research Unit, University of Kent, Canterbury.

Cambridge Economic Policy Group. (1980) 'Urban and regional policy', *Cambridge Economic Policy Review*, 6, 2, 1–85.

Cameron, G. C. (ed.) (1980) *The Future of the British Conurbations*, Longman, London.

Chisholm, M. (ed.) (1972) *Resources for Britain's Future*, Penguin, Harmondsworth.

Cloke, P. J. (1977) 'An Index of rurality for England and Wales', *Regional Studies*, 11, 31–46.

Coombes, M. G., J. S. Ditton, J. B. Goddard, S. Openshaw and P. J. Taylor (1982) 'Functional Regions for the Population Census of Great Britain', in D. J. Herbert and R. J. Johnston (eds), *Geography and the Urban Environment*, Wiley, Chichester.

Cotgrove, S. (1982) *Catastrophe or Cornucopia*, Wiley, Chichester.

Department of Health and Social Security (1978), *Medical Manpower: The Next 20 Years*, HMSO, London.

Dicken, P. (1982) 'The industrial structure and the geography of manufacturing', in Johnston and Doornkamp (1982).

Doling, J. (1982) 'Housing finance and the British city', *Area*, 14, 33–36.

Donnison, D. and P. Soto (1980) *The Good City*, Heinemann, London.

Dunn, M. *et al*. (1981) *Rural Housing: Competition and Choice*, Allen & Unwin, London.

Eyles, J., D. M. Smith and K. J. Woods (1982) 'Spatial resource allocation and state practice: the death of health service planning in London', *Regional Studies*, 16, 239, 53.

Fischhoff, B., S. Lichenstein and P. Slovic (1982) *Acceptable Risk*, Cambridge University Press, Cambridge.

Fothergill, S. and G. Gudgin (1982) *Unequal Growth: Urban and Regional Employment Change in the UK*, Heinemann, London.

GB Department of Transport (1976) *Transport Policy: A Consultation Document*, 2 vols, HMSO, London.

GB Department of Transport (1977) *Transport Policy*, Cmnd 6836, HMSO, London.

GB Department of Transport (1979) *National Travel Survey*, 1975/76 Report, HMSO, London.

GB Department of Transport (1982) *Transport Statistics Great Britain 1971–1981*, HMSO, London.

GB Department of Transport (1983) *Railway Finances*, Report of the Committee chaired by Sir David Serpell, HMSO, London.

Goddard, J. B. and I. J. Smith (1978) 'Changes in corporate control in the British urban system, 1972–1977', *Environment and Planning A*, 9, 1073–84.

Gough, I. (1983) 'Thatcherism and the Welfare State', in S. Hall and M. Jacques (eds), *The Politics of Thatcherism*, Lawrence & Wishart, London.

Hall, P. *et al*. (1973) *The Containment of Urban England*, Allen & Unwin, London.

Hall, P. (1981) 'The geography of the fifth Kondratieff cycle', *New Society*, 26 March, 535–7.

Hart, J. T. (1971) 'The inverse case law', *Lancet*, i, 405–12.

Hechter, M. (1975) *Internal Colonialism*, Routledge & Kegan Paul, London.

Henderson, R. A. (1980) 'An analysis of closures amongst Scottish manufacturing plants between 1966 and 1975', *Scottish Journal of Political Economy*, 27, 2, 152–74.

Hibbs, J. (1982) 'Transport without Politics . . .? A study of the scope for competitive markets in road, rail and air', *Hobart Paper*, 95, The Institute for Economic Affairs, London.

Hoare, A. G. (1983) *The Location of Industry in Britain*, Cambridge University Press, Cambridge.

Ince, M. (1982) *Energy Policy*, Pluto Press, Nottingham.

Jessop, B. (1982) *The Capitalist State*, Martin Robertson, Oxford.

Johnston, R. J. (1979a) *Political, Electoral and Spatial Systems*, The University Press, Oxford.

Johnston, R. J. (1979b) 'The spatial impact of fiscal changes in Britain: regional policy in reverse', *Environment and Planning A*, 11, 1439–44.

Johnston, R. J. (1982) *Geography and The State*, Macmillan, London.

Johnston, R. J. (1982) 'And the future?', in Johnston and Doornkamp (1982).

Johnston, R. J. and J. C. Doornkamp (eds) (1982) *The Changing Geography of The United Kingdom*, Methuen, London.

Keeble, D. (1976) *Industrial Location and Planning in The United Kingdom*, Methuen, London.

Keeble, D. (1977) 'Spatial policy in Britain: regional or urban?', *Area*, 9, 1, 3–8.

Keeble, D. (1978) 'Industrial decline in the inner city and conurbation', *Transactions of the Institute of British Geographers*, NS, 3, 1, 101–14.

Keeble, D. (1980a) 'South East England', chs 4–6 in G. Manners, D. Keeble, B. Rodgers and K. Warren, *Regional Development in Britain*, Wiley, London.

Keeble, D. (1980b) 'Industrial decline, regional policy and the urban–rural manufacturing shift in the United Kingdom', *Environment and Planning A*, 12, 8, 945–62.

Kirby, A. M. (1982a) 'Education, institutions and the local state', in R. Flowerdew (ed.), *Institutions and Geographic Patterns*, Croom Helm, London.

Kirby, A. M. (1982b) *The Politics of Location*, Methuen, London.

Knox, P. L. (1979) 'Medical deprivation, area deprivation and public policy', *Social Science and Medicine*, 13D, 111–21.

Knox, P. L. (1982a) *Urban Social Geography*, Longman, London.

Knox, P. L. (1982b) 'Living in the United Kingdom', in Johnston and Doornkamp (eds).

Knox, P. L. and M. Pacione (1980) 'Locational behaviour, place preferences and the inverse care law in the distribution of primary medical care', *Geoforum*, 11, 43–55.

Lansley, D. (1979) *Housing and Public Policy*, Croom Helm, London.

Law, C. M. (1981) *British Regional Development Since World War I*, Methuen, London.

Leach, G. *et al*. (1979) *A Low Energy Strategy for the UK*, IIED, London.

Mabey, R. (1981) *The Common Ground*, Hutchinson, London.

McKinley, R. D. and R. Little (1978) 'A foreign-policy model of the distribution of British bilateral aid, 1960–70', *British Journal of Political Science*, 8, 312–32.

Macrory, R. (ed.) (1981) *Nuclear Power: The Legal and Constitutional Issues*, Imperial College Centre for Environment and Technology, London.

Madgwick, P. and R. Rose (eds) (1982) *The Territorial Dimension in United Kingdom Politics*, Macmillan, London.

Manners, G. (1981) *Coal in Britain: An Uncertain Future*, Allen & Unwin, London.

Manners, G., D. Keeble, B. Rodgers and K. Warren (1980) *Regional Development in Britain*, 2nd edn, Wiley, Chichester.

Martin, R. (1982) 'Britain's slump: the regional anatomy of job loss,' *Area*, 14, 4, 257–64.

Massey, D. (1979) 'In what sense a regional problem?', *Regional Studies*, 13, 2, 233–43.

Massey, D. and R. Meegan (1982) *The Anatomy of Job Loss*, Methuen, London.

Merrett, S. (1979) *State Housing in Britain*, Routledge & Kegan Paul, London.

Merrett, S. (1982) *Owner-Occupation in Britain*, Routledge & Kegan Paul, London.

Moore, B., J. Rhodes and P. Tyler (1977) 'The Impact of regional policy in the 1970s', *CES Review*, 1, 67–77.

Moseley, M. J. (1979) *Accessibility: The Rural Challenge*, Methuen, London.

Nash, C. A. (1982) *Economics of Public Transport*, Longman, London.

Newby, H. (1979) *Green and Pleasant Land?*, Penguin, Harmondsworth.

Newton, K. (1976) 'Community performance in Britain', *Current Sociology*, 26, 49–86.

Norcliffe, G. B. and A. G. Hoare (1982) 'Enterprize Zone policy for the Inner City: a review and preliminary assessment', *Area*, 14, 4, 265–74.

Oakey, R. P., A. T. Thwaites and P. A. Nash (1980) 'The regional distribution of innovative manufacturing establishments in Britain', *Regional Studies*, 14, 3, 235–53.

O'Connor, J. (1973) *The Fiscal Crisis of the State*, St Martin's Press, New York.

Odell, P. R. (1979) 'Oil and gas exploration and exploitation in the North Sea', in E. M. Borghese and N. Ginsburg (eds), *The Ocean Yearbook, 1*, University of Chicago Press, Chicago.

Openshaw, S. and P. Stedman (1982) 'On the geography of a worst case nuclear attack on the population of Britain', *Political Geography Quarterly*, 13, 263–78.

O'Riordan, T. (1981) *Environmentalism*, Pion/Methuen, London.

Outer Circle Policy Unit (1979) *The Big Public Inquiry* 14 Cambridge Terrace, London.

Palmer, S. R., P. A. West and P. Dodd (1980) 'Randomness in the RAWP formula', *Journal of Epidemiology and Community Health*, 34, 212–6.

Parry, M. L. (1982) 'The changing use of land', in R. J. Johnston and J. C. Doornkamp (eds) *The Changing Geography of The United Kingdom*, Methuen, London.

Patterson, W. C. (1977) *The Fissile Society*, Earth Resources Research Publications, London.

PEP (1976) *A Fuel Policy for Britain*, Political and Economic Planning Report, London.

Revell, D. (1982) 'Who ordered their estate', *The Guardian*, 14 May 1982.

Rose, R. (1982) *Understanding the United Kingdom*, Longman, London.

Sandbach, F. (1980) *Environment, Ideology and Policy*, Basil Blackwell, Oxford.

Sharpe, L. J. (1982) 'The Labour Party and the geography of inequality: a paradox', in D. Kavanagh (ed.), *The Politics of the Labour Party*, Allen & Unwin, London.

Shaw, J. M. (ed.) (1979) *Rural Deprivation and Planning*, Geo Books, Norwich.

Shoard, M. (1981) *The Theft of the Countryside*, Temple Smith, London.

Short, J. R. (1982a) *An Introduction to Political Geography*, Routledge & Kegan Paul, London.

Short, J. R. (1982b) *Housing in Britain: The Post-War Experience*, Methuen, London.

Short, J. R. (1984) *The Urban Arena*, Macmillan, London.

Smith, D. M. (1974) 'Who gets what where and how: a welfare focus for Human Geography', *Geography*, 59, 289–97.

Smith, D. M. (1977) *Human Geography: A Welfare Approach*, Edward Arnold, London.

Smith, D. M. (1979) *Where the Grass is Greener*, Penguin, Harmondsworth.

Spence, N. A. (ed.) (1982) *British Cities: An Analysis of Urban Change*, Pergamon Press, Oxford.

Spooner, D. (1980) *Mining and Regional Development*, Oxford University Press, Oxford.

Starkie, D. (1982) *The Motorway Age – Road and Traffic Policies in Post-War Britain*, Pergamon Press, Oxford.

Stott, M. and P. Taylor (1981) *The Nuclear Controversy*, Town and Country Planning Association, London.

Taylor, P. J. (1979) 'The changing geography of representation in Britain', *Area*, 11, 289–94.

Taylor, P. J. (1982) 'A materialist framework for political geography', *Transactions, Institute of British Geographers*, NS7, 15–34.

Taylor, P. J. (1982) 'The changing political map', in Johnston and Doornkamp (1982).

Wells, G. (1979) 'Highway and transportation planning in England', *Transportation*, 8(2), 125–40.

Woollett, S. (1981) *Alternative Rural Services – A Community Initiatives Manual*, National Council for Voluntary Organizations, London.

Index of Authors, Politicians, etc.

Index of Subjects

Figures *in italic* relate to tables.